Praise for *True Spirituality*
Previously titled *Living on the Edge*

"A clarifying breakthrough from God's Word, which provides a spiritual compass for anyone hungry for purpose and direction. *Living on the Edge* clearly identifies God's timeless path for spiritual growth. It's amazingly relevant and applicable across the full spectrum of one's spiritual pilgrimage."

—RICK WARREN, pastor of Saddleback Church,
author of the international bestseller *The Purpose Driven Life*

"Do you have faith to believe that your very best spiritual days are in front of you? Don't read this sitting down—get on your face, then on your feet."

—JAMES MACDONALD, senior pastor of Harvest Bible Chapel,
Bible teacher at Walk in the Word

"I have seen up close Chip Ingram's passion for making authentic disciples. His gift of teaching the truths of God's Word helps believers grow to maturity. Whether you're stuck, struggling, or longing for a deeper walk with Christ, let me encourage you to consider Chip a trusted guide."

—STEVE DOUGLASS, president of Campus Crusade for Christ

"Chip has gifted the church with a biblical and motivational pathway for pursuing God's dream for your life. The encouraging tools in these pages will help you grasp what you have been reaching for. If you are searching for more in your walk with Jesus, I recommend you begin here."

—DR. JACK GRAHAM,
pastor of Prestonwood Baptist Church

"Amen! This book ignites my passion! Jesus said go make disciples, not decisions. My good friend Chip Ingram has given us a biblical, practical, and relevant pathway to achieving spiritual maturity."

—Dr. Tony Evans, senior pastor of Oak Cliff Bible
Fellowship, president of the Urban Alternative

"I found this book to be compelling, profound, and yet extremely practical. I wish I had it earlier in my walk."

—Gregg Dedrick, former president of Kentucky Fried Chicken

"Seventeen years ago, I accepted a calling for the second half of my life to work on transforming the latent energy in American Christianity into Active Energy. Chip Ingram's splendid new book, *Living on the Edge,* is focused directly on that mission. All the research indicates that the task of our time is helping Christians live more like Christians. It is the 'next steps' for believers in Halftime—the key to Finishing Well."

—Bob Buford, author of *Halftime* and *Finishing Well,*
founder and chairman of Leadership Network

"This book is a fun, stimulating, easy read. It is like having a conversation with a good friend who wants you to step up and receive everything God has in store for you."

—Gary J. Daichendt, former executive vice president
of worldwide operations, Cisco Systems

"Chip has managed to cut through all the Christian clutter and get straight to the meat of the matter. When all is said and done, all the fillers are just that—fillers. Read this book: it will meet you where the rubber meets the road."

—Michael Youssef, PhD; author of *You Want Me to Do What?*

"*Living on the Edge* is a pertinent book for the contemporary church. Chip writes with the deep conviction that spiritual maturity is the greatest need in the world today. And he faithfully offers us a biblical compass toward it. I particularly love his insight on full surrender."

—Reverend Edmund Chan, senior pastor of
Covenant Evangelical Free Church, Singapore

"I've always said life is all about relationships. My friend Chip Ingram agrees, and in *Living on the Edge,* he describes how Romans chapter 12 addresses the five critical relationships everyone must master. Chip's practical, personal, and memorable lessons will help lead you to renewing your mind and cause you to live the authentic Christian life God has always intended for us."

—Les Steckel, veteran NFL coach and president/
CEO of Fellowship of Christian Athletes

"I praise God for using Chip to write this book, which is biblically centered in content and application. The result—power in transformation."

—Peter Tan'Chi, senior pastor of
Christ's Commission Fellowship, Philippines

true spirituality

Becoming a Romans 12 Christian

CHIP INGRAM

HOWARD BOOKS
A DIVISION OF SIMON & SCHUSTER, INC.
New York • Nashville • London • Toronto • Sydney • New Delhi

Published by Howard Books,
A division of Simon & Schuster, Inc.
1230 Avenue of the Americas, New York, NY 10020
www.howardpublishing.com

Living on the Edge © 2009 Chip Ingram

First Howard Books trade paperback edition January 2011

This Howard Books revised trade paperback edition August 2013

Previously titled *Living on the Edge*

The Library of Congress has cataloged the hardcover edition as follows:

Ingram, Chip, 1954–
    Living on the edge : dare to experience true spirituality / Chip Ingram.
        p.   cm.
    ISBN 978-1-4391-3731-4 (hardcover)
        1. Christian life.   2. Christian life—Biblical teaching.   3. Bible.
N.T. Romans—Commentaries.   I. Title.
    BV4501.3.I55 2009
    248.4—dc22   2009017084

ISBN 978-1-4391-3731-4
ISBN 978-1-4391-9052-4 (pbk)
ISBN 978-1-4767-2763-9 (rev pbk)
ISBN 978-1-4391-5534-9 (ebook)
20 19 18 17 16 15 14 13 12 11

For information regarding special discounts for bulk purchases, please contact: Simon & Schuster Special Sales at 1-866-506-1949 or business@simonandschuster.com.

The Simon & Schuster Speakers Bureau can bring authors to your live event. For more information or to book an event, contact the Simon & Schuster Speakers Bureau at 1-866-248-3049 or visit our website at www.simonspeakers.com.

Cover design by Lighthouse Marketing • Marietta, GA

Scripture quotations marked NASB are taken from the New American Standard Bible, © 1960, 1962, 1963, 1968, 1971, 1972, 1973, 1975, 1977 by The Lockman Foundation. Used by permission. Scripture quotations marked NIV are taken from the Holy Bible, New International Version®. Copyright © 1973, 1978, 1984 by International Bible Society. Used by permission of Zondervan. All rights reserved. Scripture quotations marked GNT are from the Good News Translation in Today's English Version—Second Edition. Copyright © 1992 by American Bible Society. Used by Permission.

Special type treatment in quoted scripture has been added by author for emphasis.

To Annie and Theresa . . . your *tireless hands*
and *praying hearts* made this book possible.

Contents

Acknowledgments

This book is the culmination of a thirty-six-year journey. It is not so much something that I have written as it is what God has scripted in me since the summer of 1972 when I opened the Bible for the first time and read Romans chapter 12.

How can I ever thank the Fellowship of Christian Athletes, Dave Marshall, the Navigators, my sister, Dallas Seminary, Country Bible Country Church, and Santa Cruz Bible Church for their mentoring, love, reproof, and instruction? Closer to home, I have lived with an amazing r12 wife and r12 children, whose passionate pursuit of Christ demanded authenticity from me and produced transformation in me.

I want to thank Walk Thru the Bible and a gathering of pastors in Lagos, Nigeria, for being the catalyst for the r12 paradigm.

I want to thank the amazing team at Living on the Edge who honed the message with me, created video, audio, e-learning, online coaching, a social network, and spiritual resources to help Christians across the globe to "live like Christians" (Greg, Vicki, Linda, Stir, Sandy, and their teams).

I am especially indebted to the wise counsel and strategic insight of Andrew and "his friends" Lance, Bill, Brett, Rob, and Mark.

I want to thank John Howard for his belief in the project and his amazing patience to wait on God's timing. Special thanks to Simon & Schuster for their flexibility and willingness to create a ministry edition and overcome deadline obstacles to get this book to press.

I want to thank Curtis Yates and Yates & Yates, Inc., for their perseverance with me and their genuine commitment to ministry.

Finally, I want to thank Annie, who typed and edited the manuscript three times, made invaluable suggestions, worked literally around the clock to hit the deadline, and modeled Romans 12:10–11 through the process: "Be devoted to one another in brotherly love. Honor one another above yourselves. Never be lacking in zeal, but keep your spiritual fervor, serving the Lord."

I want to thank our Monday-night Bible study of young professionals, who showed me what Romans 12 looks like with skin on when you're twenty-five and single.

Before We Begin

Welcome to *True Spirituality*.

You are joining millions of fellow travelers all over the world who have read, listened to, or studied my teachings on "Becoming a Romans 12 Christian." Their testimonies of God's power and presence in their lives fuel my passion to invite you to come join us and go deeper with Jesus in this book—*True Spirituality*.

If you're looking for secret formulas, gimmicks, quick fixes, or easy steps, this book is *not* for you. This book and this journey *are* for those who long for genuine, intimate, *True Spirituality*.

1. Is This Book for You?

*The answer is **YES** if . . .*

- You are spiritually hungry.
- You long for more God.
- You are tired of status quo Christianity.
- You are spiritually stuck.
- You long to break free from some habitual sin.
- You are ready for a challenge.
- You are discipling others.

2. What Is This Book About?

First of all, this book is not about being religious, keeping rules, developing programs, church growth, self-actualization, or spiritual formulas for success. Rather, it's about helping you answer five of the most important questions in your life.

- How do you give God what He wants the most?
- How do you get God's best for your life?
- How do you come to grips with the real you?
- How can you experience authentic community?
- How do you overcome the evil aimed at you?

In other words, this book is about *living on the edge;* it's about stepping out with courage as you dare to experience true spirituality.

3. Why This Book NOW?

Recent research has shown that church programs are not producing mature Christians. Sincere Christians have tried lots of dead-end, theologically flawed, and quick-fix spiritual approaches that have left them . . .

- Performing and exhausted
- Feeling guilty and ashamed
- A prisoner of false expectations
- Disappointed and disillusioned
- Angry and bitter
- Leaving the church
- Quietly going through religious motions with little sense of God's power or presence.

4. How Is This Book Different?

This book provides an actual *profile* for becoming more like Jesus every day. The profile is . . .

- *Biblical:* an exposition of Romans 12; God's executive summary of the profile of an authentic Christ-follower.
- *Relational:* spiritual maturity is achieved by growing in five key relationships, not by keeping rules.
- *Grace-based:* a Romans 12 disciple grows out of an understanding of Romans 1–11; it's not performance-oriented.
- *Faith-focused:* spiritual maturity is achieved by learning to trust God, not "try harder."
- *Practical:* discipleship provides the "how-to" of spiritual growth, not simply the ideal.
- *Measurable:* Romans 12 provides specific metrics to help you determine if you are making spiritual progress.

You also need to know that this book is a "doorway," not a final destination. As you read, you will be launched on a journey toward becoming a Christian who is living on the edge. At the end of each chapter you'll find resources and questions to help you personally process and apply what God is doing in your life.

At the end of each section of the book you will find a page called B.I.O. While Romans 12 is the profile of a disciple, B.I.O. is the pathway. *BIO* is a term synonymous with life and represents three regular practices that help you live out Romans 12 in your everyday life.

- B=Come **Before God** daily: Meeting with Him personally through His word and prayer to enjoy His presence, receive His direction, and follow His will.

- I=Do Life **In Community** weekly: Structuring your week to connect personally in safe relationships that provide love, support, transparency, challenge, and accountability.
- O=Be **On Mission** 24/7: Cultivating a mindset to "live out" Jesus' love for others through acts of sacrifice and service at home, work, play, and church.

On our interactive Web site (LivingontheEdge.org), you will discover clear spiritual pathways to help you grow. Here, you will be able to share your journey with others, receive personal coaching to make it over barriers, and be given practical tools to help you help others.

Romans 12 is the START HERE for the Christian life. It's not everything, but if you're stuck—START HERE; if you are a new believer and unsure how to grow—START HERE; if you are a mature believer and are looking for a pathway to disciple others—START HERE.

Are you ready for the journey of your lifetime?

---

* *NOTE TO PASTORS: There is a special message for you at the end of the book on page 271. Jump to that now; then come back and join the rest of us.*

My r12 Journey

My simple question was met with blank stares and silence.

I was speaking to a large gathering of pastors in Nigeria about the purpose of the church as defined in Matthew 28:19: "Go and make disciples of all nations, baptizing them in the name of the Father and of the Son and of the Holy Spirit . . ."

So, I had asked them, *What is a disciple?* I didn't want a definition, but I wanted them to tell me what an authentic follower of Christ looks like. Just like their cobelievers I had spoken to around the world, they struggled to give a clear, measurable, biblical profile of a disciple of Jesus Christ.

It was then I had one of those amazing experiences where God puts things in your mouth that aren't in your notes. I said, "If there was a giant server up in heaven and you logged on to www.heaven .com/disciple, do you know what would come up on your laptop?" They all leaned forward in anticipation and I was praying silently that the answer would be as profound as the question I had not planned on asking. Then out of my mouth I heard, "Becoming a Romans 12 Christian."

At the Spirit's prompting I asked them to close their workbooks and open their Bibles to Romans 12. It was the first chapter I had ever memorized, more than thirty years earlier, the first Christian commentary I had ever studied, and I had taught this passage many times before, but never in the way I shared it with them.

That was the beginning of God's orchestration of my life to take all I have done in the last twenty-five years of ministry and ignite it around my deepest passion—spiritual maturity. Below you'll see an overview of what I shared with these dear pastors and where we will be going together in the days ahead as you begin to experience *living on the edge.*

The Profile of an r12 Disciple Is . . .

SURRENDERED TO GOD (V. 1)

Therefore, I urge you, brothers, in view of God's mercy, to offer your bodies as living sacrifices, *holy and pleasing to God—this is your spiritual act of worship.*

SEPARATE FROM THE WORLD (V. 2)

Do not conform any longer to the pattern of this world, *but be transformed by the renewing of your mind. Then you will be able to test and approve what God's will is—his good, pleasing and perfect will.*

SOBER IN SELF-ASSESSMENT (VV. 3–8)

For by the grace given me I say to every one of you: Do not think of yourself more highly than you ought, but rather think of yourself with sober judgment, *in accordance with the measure of faith God has given you. Just as each of us has one body with many members, and these members do not all have the same function, so in Christ we who are many form one body, and each member belongs to all the others. We have different gifts, according to the grace given us. If a man's gift is prophesying, let him use it in pro-*

portion to his faith. If it is serving, let him serve; if it is teaching, let him teach; if it is encouraging, let him encourage; if it is contributing to the needs of others, let him give generously; if it is leadership, let him govern diligently; if it is showing mercy, let him do it cheerfully.

SERVING IN LOVE (VV. 9–13)

Love must be sincere. *Hate what is evil; cling to what is good. Be devoted to one another in brotherly love. Honor one another above yourselves. Never be lacking in zeal, but keep your spiritual fervor, serving the Lord. Be joyful in hope, patient in affliction, faithful in prayer. Share with God's people who are in need. Practice hospitality.*

SUPERNATURALLY RESPONDING TO EVIL WITH GOOD (VV. 14–21)

Bless those who persecute you; bless and do not curse. *Rejoice with those who rejoice; mourn with those who mourn. Live in harmony with one another. Do not be proud, but be willing to associate with people of low position. Do not be conceited. Do not repay anyone evil for evil. Be careful to do what is right in the eyes of everybody. If it is possible, as far as it depends on you, live at peace with everyone. Do not take revenge, my friends, but leave room for God's wrath, for it is written: "It is mine to avenge; I will repay," says the Lord. On the contrary: "If your enemy is hungry, feed him; if he is thirsty, give him something to drink. In doing this, you will heap burning coals on his head. Do not be overcome by evil, but overcome evil with good."*

The Big Picture

Romans 12 is an executive summary (the Cliffs Notes) of what a fully mature follower of Jesus looks like. It's the Apostle Paul's synthesis of Jesus' teaching on discipleship.

Note carefully:

1. *Its focus is on your relationships:*
   - Your relationship with God (v. 1)
   - Your relationship to this world's values (v. 2)
   - Your relationship with yourself (vv. 3–8)
   - Your relationship with believers (vv. 9–13)
   - Your relationship with unbelievers (vv. 14–21)

2. *It's about grace.* Romans 12 follows eleven chapters that give us the clearest and most detailed account of Christ's work on our behalf.

3. *It's practical and measurable.* Romans 12 is filled with specific commands (to be fulfilled through the Spirit's power) that set the bar for maturity in each of those five relationships.

In the days ahead we will walk through this passage together. You will gain a very clear picture of who God is creating you to be and how to cooperate with His supernatural work of transformation.

How It All Started for Me

It's always good to see that you're not alone in your struggles, doubts, fears, and occasional failures. So let me start our journey with my story. Throughout the book I'll come back to my story, if for no other reason than to show how God works in varying stages of all our journeys.

I didn't grow up as a Christian. I thought I was; I went to church, believed in God intellectually, had a good, moral family, but absolutely no concept of a personal relationship with the living God. It wasn't that I was closed to the idea of God, in fact I can remember as a small boy having what I would call a "God experience" that strangely but briefly impacted my life.

I was an altar boy at the age of eight or nine years old. I would carry the cross down the aisle with the minister behind me as the service started. I remember the huge A-frame building with a cross that went from floor to ceiling surrounded by stained glass. It was the eight o'clock service and the sun came through the glass in such a way that light reflected off the altar, pointing back to the base of the cross. I was a very young kid with no theological understanding, but as I sat through that service and stared at that cross, thoughts I had never considered cascaded through my mind.

I wonder what God is like? What would the God who created everything want with my one little life? These thoughts gently pressed upon my consciousness as my eyes were fixated on the light at the base of the cross. It was the first time I had a sense of God's presence with a budding awareness that He was personal and real. It's hard to explain, but I remember telling my mother and father after the service that I wanted to be the altar boy at the eight o'clock service every week from then on. Looking back, it was clearly the Holy Spirit beginning to woo my heart and manifest His presence at a level I could understand. The inner confirmation of being wanted and loved was overwhelming—I intuitively knew it was related somehow to what occurred on the cross. That's all I could get my mind around as an eight-year-old; but it was powerful, it was real, and I was drawn to know and serve this God who made me.

Unfortunately, my newfound spiritual passion was short-lived. I grew up in a church that did not believe in the Bible or in having a personal relationship with Jesus Christ. The church was beautiful, the pageantry was majestic, and the form was highly structured. We read our prayers, we said the right things, we fulfilled our religious duty, and then we went home. To say that my church experience was a compartmentalized segment of my life would be an understatement. It's all I knew and it was what I observed in my home and with other significant adults. In fact, by the time I was a preteen I was able to go through the entire service by rote memory and simultaneously relive mental video clips of classic NBA matchups from the day before.

It was not that this church was purposely irreverent or irrelevant. We were simply a religious group of people in complete denial of the God of the Bible, even though we used biblical passages and historic forms of worship to address our spiritual need. What was most disturbing to a young and naive person like myself was that there was absolutely no expectation that what we did on Sunday would have any impact on how we lived the rest of the week.

By the time I was a teenager the hypocrisy and irrelevancy of my church experience began to make me cast severe doubts on the reality of God. I wanted to believe, but the older I got, the less interested I became in going through the religious motions and pretending and saying things that no one lived or believed. When I was sixteen, I vividly remember thinking to myself, *All this religious stuff is just whitewash that these adults have told us kids to keep us "in line" morally until we get old enough to discover there is no Easter Bunny, Santa Claus, or God.* It was all a carefully crafted spiritual camouflage. I had the distinct feeling that I was being conned and I didn't like it. As a result, I disengaged from church and God and did not believe either offered me any real help to find purpose and happiness in life.

Like many in my generation in the late sixties and early seventies, I was taught that happiness and fulfillment are the product of being successful. My father instilled in me at an early age the importance of setting clear goals, developing a strategy to achieve them, and then working harder than anyone else if I wanted to experience success and happiness. It's hard to become a workaholic by the seventh grade, but looking back, somehow I managed. I set goals with regard to sports, school, girls, and then worked like crazy to fulfill them.

I was that crazy kid shoveling snow off the driveway to shoot baskets in the middle of the winter. My dream was to get a college basketball scholarship and someday be famous, rich, and happy. I knew I was pretty small and so I figured college would be as far as I could go athletically, so I worked hard to get the good grades that would set me up for future success. Money also seemed to be something that was pretty important if you were serious about being successful. So by the time I was twelve, I had two paper routes, my own lawn business, and figured out how to lend my parents three thousand dollars at about 6 percent interest when they wanted to buy a piece of land behind our house.

Life was about me. Life was about my goals, my dreams, and my success that someday would make me fulfilled and happy. That was the mantra I believed and pursued. And then something strange happened the night I graduated from high school.

I graduated near the top of my class, earned a basketball scholarship to a small liberal arts school, had earned a few awards along the way, and had a pretty girl on my arm. Although I certainly didn't achieve all my goals, I had achieved the majority of them and was ready to launch into the next season of my life "to achieve the next set of goals."

I will never forget what happened the night I graduated from high school. It was a spiritually defining moment in my life that I never expected. About twenty of us were sitting in an empty apartment in a circle passing a joint around and sharing stories from high school. When it came my turn, I chose to pass it on, not out of any religious conviction, but for fear that putting anything in my body might limit my chances for future athletic success. Sitting next to me was a girl named Jackie who had befriended me in high school. She was one of the first girls whom I had experienced a real friendship with and had no romantic inclination toward her (in view of the size and the strength of her boyfriend). Because of our friendship, we often talked very deeply and I remember her being very insightful. She probably never knew it, but she said something to me that night that changed the course of my life.

"Well, Chip, you must be really happy tonight. You've got it made. You have a scholarship to college, a pretty girl, you won lots of awards, and have a really great future ahead of you. How does it feel to be so successful?" Although she meant it as a compliment, I realized I had rarely taken any time to examine how I felt. And in that moment I felt anything but fulfilled and happy. Rather, I felt empty, alone, and this foreboding sense of futility. I've always been a pretty logical person and so I immediately began to play out the scenario that I had just experienced. I had set clear goals, I worked like crazy, learned how to charm people to fulfill my own selfish needs, and I had finally arrived . . . I was successful!

But what I didn't expect was how empty success would be. In my mind that night driving home, I began to extrapolate the future goals I had mentally set for my future. *Okay,* I said to myself, *you go to college, become a lawyer, make lots of money, marry a beautiful girl, have three beautiful kids, live in the suburbs, drive an expensive car, wear two-hundred-dollar suits, and become a leader in the community—that's what success will look like in the next ten to fifteen years.* And then I thought, *I will work like crazy to accomplish those things and I will . . . feel as empty then as I do now. There must be more to life than this.*

Before I went to bed that night, I sat on my bed and looked out my bedroom window. It was a night filled with stars and I began asking questions that I had never seriously considered.

I wonder . . . why am I here? I wonder, what I'm supposed to do with my life? I wonder if there really is a God who exists; and if so, what does He want from me?

I vividly remember staring out that window and praying the first honest adult prayer of my life:

"God, if You exist, show Yourself to me. If You really are real, You must be powerful enough to reveal Yourself to me in a way that I can understand. And if You created all that there is and You are real, I will do whatever You want me to do. But if You're not real, if there is no God, if this is all there is . . . I'm going to live like hell, die young, and have as much fun as I can squeeze in this futile thing called life."

My success had only led me to a dead end. My paradigm was shattered. Being successful and achieving goals (though exhilarating in the process) did not have the power to bring peace or purpose to my life.

A New Beginning

A few weeks after I prayed that prayer, I found myself at a summer camp with the Fellowship of Christian Athletes. A delay in a summer job and the offer by a coach at our school to pay my way landed me in a new and strange world. I was given a Bible and a T-shirt, and was dropped into an environment that I did not know existed. People talked about God and Jesus as though He was a real person. College and professional athletes talked about their relationship with Jesus in the same breath as their relationship with their wives or children. A man got up each morning and read a portion out of the Bible and explained it in a way that actually made sense.

We played sports most of the day and I had a blast. Fun, sports, authenticity, and the camaraderie with fellow athletes connected to having a personal relationship with Jesus was completely new to me. To be very honest, my past religious experience made me more than a little skeptical. I actually thought these people were going to try to indoctrinate me and make me a "Jesus freak." We were supposed to read the Bible every morning, but I figured this was one of their ways to brainwash me, so I refused to open it the first three days.

But something happened on day number four. I decided to open the Bible and at least see what it said since I couldn't deny the reality of these people's sincerity or their love for one another. It was obvious they had something I didn't, and I remember the prayer that I had prayed in my bedroom late that night after high school graduation: "God, if you exist show me in a way that I can understand."

So partly out of peer pressure and partly out of genuine curiosity, I opened the easy-to-read New Testament that I was given and read what it said at the top of the page:

> *So then, my friends, because of God's great mercy to us I appeal to you: Offer yourselves as a living sacrifice to God, dedicated to his service and pleasing to him. This is the true worship that you should offer.*
>
> *Do not conform yourselves to the standards of this world, but let God transform you inwardly by a complete change of your mind. Then you will be able to know the will of God—what is good and is pleasing to him and is perfect.*
>
> —ROMANS 12:1–2 GNT

I had been asking the question: "If God exists, what does He really want from me?" I assumed from my childhood church experience that He wanted me to keep a bunch of rules (most of which I didn't like!). I thought He wanted me to attend boring religious services where the people didn't believe what they were saying and certainly didn't live what they "believed." I assumed it was a life that would be totally irrelevant to anything meaningful to me with regard to the goals and dreams that were on my heart. To top it off, I didn't know what God really wanted, but after watching some Christian TV, I figured He was probably after my money.

Forgive my skepticism, and my irreverent view of God; but that is what I honestly thought up until the time that I went to this camp and opened the Bible for myself. Now, seated on the grassy lawn of a small college in Ohio with seven hundred other athletes, I read a passage that answered the very question I had asked God just a week earlier: "What do you really want from me?" And He answered, "All I want is you!"

I do understand that Romans 12:1 is not a salvation passage; by that, I mean this passage does not teach someone how to enter into a relationship with Jesus and receive forgiveness of their sins. But God used this passage to help me come to grips with what God indeed wanted from me . . . and wants from all of His children.

It's not our religious activities, it's not keeping rules, it's not being a dutiful soldier fulfilling a cause. He wants our lives and our hearts in intimate, joyful, relationship with Him.

Later that week I would hear the good news of the Gospel of Jesus Christ. I would come to understand that there was nothing I could do to earn God's favor, but that Christ had died in my place to forgive my sin and this free gift could only be received by faith. I didn't understand much, but I did understand my desperate need for a Savior and the clear teaching of Scripture that says Christ paid for my sin once and for all.

> *For it is by grace you have been saved, through faith—and this not from yourselves, it is the gift of God—not by works, so that no one can boast.*
>
> —EPHESIANS 2:8–9

Unfortunately, in many books and in many church services, what I just shared (the Gospel) becomes not only the beginning but the end of the message. The great majority of Christians have been taught that life is about coming to know Christ personally, being saved, being good, and then helping other people "get saved." Before long, they become a part of the religious machinery whose primary goal is to help more people enter the kingdom of God.

Please do not get me wrong: evangelism is very important and leading people to Christ is at the top of God's priority list. But the second half of the message has been sorely neglected: the part about God's dream that you become a precious and cherished son or daughter living in deep union with Him.

God's dream and plan for each of His children is not about rules or religious activity but about relationship. God's desire is not for our performance, but for us to learn to live out of the grace and favor we already possess. God's primary agenda is to make us more and more like His Son so that we enjoy and love Him and others the way He loves them.

This life can be yours. I have tasted it and watched countless other ordinary people like you and me experience it. My passion is that you will dare to step out to the dramatic and exciting edges of life—the place in life where you are in sync with God and feel alive and vibrant and filled with purpose. And though the edge is a bit scary at times, this life is filled with passion, risk, and reward. So, fasten your spiritual seatbelt as we embark on a journey that will lead you to the *edge*.

true
spirituality

.

How to Give God What He Wants the Most

SURRENDERED TO GOD
ROMANS 12:1

The whole outlook of mankind might be changed
if we could all believe that we dwell under a friendly sky
and that the God of heaven, though exalted in power and majesty,
is eager to be friends with us.[1]
—A. W. Tozer

.

CHAPTER ONE

What does God really want from you?

Come to me, all you who are weary and burdened,
and I will give you rest.[2]
—*Jesus of Nazareth*

Well, I'd like to say that my life was completely changed, my problems were put behind me, and my new relationship with Christ was one of countless victory after victory; but I can't. My life did change. God did a radical work in my heart and planted a new set of desires within me. No one told me I had to read the Bible, but I couldn't put it down. I read it at night and in the morning with a sense that the living God was speaking directly to me. No one told me I had to stop "doing this or that," but somehow God changed my desires . . . and the sin that I once enjoyed became repulsive. I had peace in my heart and often a song on my lips. I was free. I was motivated and wanted to share the love that I now experienced with everyone.

New Life/New Struggles

But my new life also introduced new struggles. Although some sins quickly vanished, others seemed impossible to overcome. I was very fortunate to have some mature Christians enter my life shortly after my conversion and teach me how to live the Christian life. Little by little, I learned how to get to know God and understand His Word so He could talk back to me. The early days were filled with a joy that I'd never known and followed by tests that I had never imagined.

As I read through my New Testament in the mornings and talked with God about school, basketball, and girls, I soon learned that His opinion about how to "do" life was a little bit different from mine. Jesus was certainly my Savior, but He was far from the Lord of my life. I was growing and confused. I felt such joy in my new relationship with Christ, but I didn't want anyone telling me what to do. Unconsciously I began to compartmentalize my faith (just like I observed in the church of my childhood) and took a salad-bar approach to God's commands. The ones that I liked and seemed reasonable I obeyed; and the ones that I disliked and seemed unreasonable I chose to disregard.

As I look back, it was a crazy way to live. I read my Bible in the mornings and had a wonderful time with God, only to experience extreme remorse and guilt later in the day as I engaged in activities that violated the Holy Spirit living within me. I looked forward to Thursday-night Bible study, where our campus ministry would crowd into a small living room to sing songs, share our hearts, and experience God's presence in a powerful way.

On Friday and Saturday nights I would load in the car with four or five players on the basketball team and hit every bar in Wheeling, West Virginia. I was the one with the social skills, so I was appointed the designated "introducer" to the good-looking girls. Often getting home in the wee hours of the morning, I would miss church, feel guilty, ask for forgiveness, receive it, and continue on with this schizophrenic Christian life.

Though I didn't show it, I was miserable. Over time the joy of the Lord began to fade as I constantly violated my conscience, and even the sin I once enjoyed lost its ability to satisfy, as it was always accompanied with guilt and shame—now that I had the Holy Spirit living in me.

It was about two and a half years into my journey with Christ that God had me revisit those two very important questions: "What is it that God really wants from me the most? And how do I give it to Him?" It was these two questions that brought me to a point of seriously reexamining my relationship with the living God.

Giving God What He Really Wants

As I was reading through the Scripture one day with a group of guys my age, I realized that my double, compartmentalized life had never been God's intent. He wanted *me*—all of me! The missing power and the absent joy could only come as I understood and applied the truth of Romans 12:1 . . . only when I learned about surrender.

God wanted me to surrender all that I am and all that I have in submission to Him. He wanted to have the same place in my heart that He possesses in the universe. He wanted me to believe that He was so good, kind, and loving that I would entrust all of me to Him, knowing He had my best in mind. He wanted me to bring my dreams, my future, my girlfriend, my basketball career, my academics to Him with open palms. He wanted me to bring my everything so that He might reign in my heart as He reigns in the universe.

I cannot begin to tell you the extent of the struggle and battle I experienced in coming to a place of surrender. My view of God was so warped that I assumed to surrender to Him would mean the end of the things that I held most dear.

Surrender and fear were synonymous in my mind and heart. I was single and certainly wanted to be married someday. But I thought if I surrendered to God, He might want me to be single and I would be miserable my whole life. Or worse, He would direct me to marry some ugly girl whom I never wanted to be with. If I surrendered, He might ask me to quit basketball and send me to some strange land to be a missionary. If I surrendered, He might want me to change what I was studying to something different that I would probably hate. Over and over in my mind the issue of surrender became paramount.

As I look back, I see that it was my misunderstanding of God and the concept of surrender that destined me to be a cultural, carnal, hypocritical follower of Jesus—the very thing I had hated growing up.

I wanted to begin our journey together by sharing my story of struggling with the Christian life, because according to the best research and my personal experience, the great majority of "Christians" in the United States and around the world live in this great twilight. Believers who know and love God and yet do not experience His joy, power, or presence anywhere near the way God longs for them to know Him.

It was my misunderstanding of God and the concept of surrender that destined me to be a cultural, carnal, hypocritical follower of Jesus—the very thing I had hated growing up.

If you're tired of all the rules, all the formulas, all the religious activities, and even well-meaning church programs that promise transformation but don't deliver, I invite you to join me on a journey of grace, faith, and relationship that leads to genuine transformation. Together we'll learn what it really looks like to follow Christ and how in His power and grace, you can live a new, radical, abundant life.

In order for this to occur it will require your participation. Reading or even agreeing with what Scripture says about spiritual transformation does not make it happen. So at the end of each chapter I will provide you some key questions, assignments, and resources to help you process and apply what God is saying to you.

I use the acronym TRUST ME to remind you that what pleases God the most is our faith (Hebrews 11:6). You will be tempted to see r12 as the "bar of discipleship" that you need to achieve instead of the profile of what Christ wants to produce in your heart and relationship through His power and grace.

Don't feel compelled to answer all the questions at the end of each chapter or do all the assignments. They are there to help you hear God's voice, overcome common barriers, and cooperate with the Holy Spirit's work in your heart—not to be another list of things you need to do. The most important question you can ask at the end of each chapter (and in all circumstances for that matter) is "What does it look like to trust God? What does it look like to trust God in view of what I just read? What does it look like to trust God in my job, my relationships, my future, etc.?"

TRUST ME will walk you through a grace-oriented process to help you hear what God is saying to you. Let's get started in this first chapter on surrender:

IT'S YOUR MOVE—Become an ⊙12 Christian

God longs to speak personally to you. Take two minutes and slowly read through the TRUST ME questions and suggestions for spiritual growth. Then sit quietly for three minutes and ask God which of those questions or actions might provide a pathway that will strengthen and encourage you. Don't feel compelled to answer all the questions or do all that is suggested; listen to the Holy Spirit and follow His leading.

THINK—What part of my struggle with surrender spoke to you?

REFLECT—Why do you think that aspect of my story resonated in your heart?

UNDERSTAND—How might God be speaking to you? Are you afraid? Convicted? Relieved that others have the same struggles?

SURRENDER—Take a moment and simply tell God how you are feeling. Share your fears, relief, or honest struggles with Him. Tell Him you want to learn more and want His help to really understand what surrender is all about.

TAKE ACTION—Decide when you will read the next chapter to hear God's heart concerning surrender.

MOTIVATION—Go to the web **(LivingontheEdge.org/r12)** and watch the fourteen-minute video "How to Give God What He Wants the Most."

ENCOURAGE SOMEONE—Take one minute and pray for someone who is going through a struggle in their journey of surrender.

CHAPTER TWO

Why is it so hard
to surrender to God?

Take my yoke upon you and learn from me,
for I am gentle and humble in heart,
and you will find rest for your souls.[1]
—*Jesus of Nazareth*

I recently came across a book written by a Yale law professor titled *Risk, Reason and the Decision-Making Process.*[2] It's a compilation of case studies that is used at Harvard Business School and MIT to help graduate students learn to make excellent decisions. Although a secular resource, this book provides unusual insight into the issue of "surrender" as it relates to making major decisions about life and relationships. Let me share a couple case studies that are important for our consideration as we think about making wise decisions in our relationship to God and others.

Case Study 1

John is a thirty-two-year-old engineer who loves to go to estate sales and look for antique furniture and other potentially valuable items. One particular weekend John found himself at an estate sale in the southern part of the United States. All the items in the house were going to be sold at a single-unit price. Visitors were walking from floor to floor, examining the various antiques and pondering what bid they would make to buy all the contents of the house. John, after doing some research on the Internet, determined that the winning bid would probably be somewhere around ninety-five thousand dollars.

The house was old and in disrepair. The architecture and antiques scattered from room to room indicated it was probably built during the Civil War era. John had been a history buff for a number of years and recognized a collection of rifles from that time period.

As John continued his investigation, he proceeded downstairs into a damp basement. Using a small pocket flashlight, he sees an old roll-top desk located in the corner covered in cobwebs. As John searched through the poorly lit desk he discovers a false drawer and, in the drawer, a small leather pouch. John's heart begins to beat more quickly and his blood pressure rises as he begins to ponder what treasure he might find. John, far from being disappointed, opens the pouch and finds twenty-two very rare, pure-gold coins minted by the Confederacy during the Civil War. To his knowledge, they are likely worth millions of dollars.

Now John has to make a decision. What should he do? He has ten thousand dollars in savings. If he can sell his car, his house, and everything else he owns, he believes he can come up with the ninety-five-thousand-dollar winning bid price. But what should he do? Students at Harvard Business School and MIT now discuss this case study.

Case Study 2

Sheila is an art professor in a small community college in the Midwest. While traveling in Europe for the summer, she looks for paintings she can afford to put in her own collection. While in a small village in southern France, well off the beaten path, Sheila goes to an auction and sees a painting that looks very much like an original Picasso. It is an amazing replica, but the people at the art auction tell her it's not an original. It is deemed to be merely an extraordinary copy of Picasso's work because the signature at the bottom does not look like Picasso's signature in other works.

Sheila pulls out her magnifying glass and begins to examine the painting carefully, realizing that she may in fact be in front of a rare masterpiece. Through her reading she has learned that some of Picasso's early works had only his initials scribbled roughly. Picasso changed this after his first year of work when he began to sign his painting with his full name. If this is true, Sheila is standing in front of a priceless piece of art.

The price tag was twenty-five thousand dollars—a huge sum of money for her. But if in fact this was an original Picasso and one of the two or three believed to have been done prior to his signing his full name, she was holding one of the world's rarest pieces of art, worth millions. What should Sheila do?

The twenty-five-thousand-dollar asking price was a joke on Sheila's budget, but her heart raced and her mind began to quickly calculate what she could get for her entire collection if she sold it all to purchase this potential masterpiece. Sheila was at a crossroads. She could sell her current collection and instantly become a multimillionaire, or sell her entire collection only to discover that the painting was only a replica. What should she do?

To answer this question, one must weigh both the risk and the rewards of any decision that is to be made. Harvard and MIT graduate students are now asked to examine both case studies based on the following four questions:

1. What are the risks?
2. What are the potential rewards?
3. What would you do?
4. Why?

RISK VERSUS REWARD

The key issues in both case studies involve a number of important factors that are critical to identify and apply in order to make wise decisions. The first and most important factor centers on the issue of *truth* or authenticity—the validity of the find. If in fact the gold coins are authentic and the painting is authentic, it would be the height of foolishness for either John or Sheila not to do whatever necessary to purchase them.

The second factor revolves around the issue of *knowledge*. Both John and Sheila possess knowledge not shared by most people. John is an admitted geek with a real bent for history and as a result was able to identify not only the rifles but a number of the antiques in the house to be authentic to the Civil War period. His reading and research also informed him that in the early days of the Confederacy gold coins were minted until the economic situation changed and paper money was printed.

In the same manner, Sheila's educational background was the key to catching this potential rare find. As an art teacher, she'd studied not only Picasso's artwork but the life of Picasso himself. It was her knowledge of the subject matter and its background that set her apart from all the other observers. Great decisions demand a thorough knowledge of the issues at hand to authenticate and evaluate what level of risk is involved in making a decision. John and Sheila both had to ask and answer the question "Is this true? Do I have a masterpiece or rare set of coins worth millions or am I mistaken?" In these particular cases, their unique knowledge and background allowed them to authenticate their findings to a very high degree of probability.

The third factor is the issue of *faith* and *courage*. It's one thing to intellectually believe that you have found a Picasso painting; it's quite another to sell all of your hard-earned art collection to purchase it. The same is true for John. To be intellectually convinced that these coins are real is one thing, but to sell your home, your car, and cash in your life insurance policy is far from an intellectual decision.

I think it's obvious why these two case studies would generate a lot of excellent discussion around the issues of risk, reason, and the decision-making process. I want to come back and talk about these two case studies in just a minute; but first let's take a look at a third case study.

Case Study 3

Case study 3 is about an ancient treasure and the story goes like this:

> *The kingdom of heaven is like a treasure hidden in the field, which a man found and hid again; and from joy over it he goes and sells all that he has and buys that field. Again, the kingdom of heaven is like a merchant seeking fine pearls, and upon finding one pearl of great value, he went and sold all that he had and bought it.*
>
> —JESUS, MATTHEW 13:44–46 NASB

This ancient case study is a story that Jesus told to explain the Kingdom of heaven. In it He depicts a situation that would not be uncommon in that day. In Jesus' day people, in lieu of a 401(k), would take their treasure and hide it in a field for safekeeping. However, often they would die without their relatives knowing the location of the treasure. It was not uncommon for someone to find the treasure of another buried in a field. In this particular situation Jesus' explanation has four parts.

One, the man found a treasure of great value. Two, he covered the treasure. Three, he was delirious with joy. Four, he sold all his possessions in order to buy the treasure. And as is the case in much of Hebrew thinking and poetry, the second story is given to make the exact same point but using different specifics while emphasizing the same

principle. The story of the merchant and the one great pearl emphasizes how life in the Kingdom of God is to work. In both stories told by
Jesus, we see a picture of reckless sacrifice and wild abandonment of a
man's treasure in order to get something of far greater value. Far from
a picture of renunciation or personal sacrifice, this is a picture of reevaluation and reward.

So what do these three stories have in common? Well, let me start
by telling you that the twenty-two golden coins were in fact authentic
and John, our friend the engineer, has become extraordinarily wealthy.
In a like manner, Sheila had the faith and courage to pull the trigger on
her deepest intuition and is now in the possession of one of the rarest
Picasso paintings that has ever been discovered. She still teaches art at
her community college, but is well positioned financially for the rest of
her life.

But before we go on and examine Jesus' case study with regard to
the treasure found in a field, let me ask you a couple of important questions: "Do you feel sorry for John or Sheila?" After all, John sold all that
he owned and Sheila gave up her entire art collection and life savings.
"Do you admire them as people who are virtuous or godly?"

You may even ask me why I ask that question, but I'll get to that in
a minute. I'm assuming, like me, you're saying to yourself, why would
I think they're virtuous? The fact of the matter is they're smart. The
fact is that when I read the story of John and Sheila, the only thing
that comes to my mind is that I wish I was John and knew what he
knew in order to get what he got, or I wish I was Sheila and knew what
she knew and was where she was to get what she got. In other words,
I don't think they're virtuous or righteous or better than me; but I
do think they were smart, knowledgeable, and courageously willing
to pull the trigger on what they knew in order to cash in on the big
prize.

Now, with that in mind, I want you to look afresh at the case study
Jesus gives His first-century listeners. In it, He explains for us how life

with God really works—how to get the very best from God and how to achieve this life of abundance and joy that Christians so often talk about. Jesus' case study teaches: Total commitment is the channel through which God's best and biggest blessings flow.

COMMITMENT/SURRENDER

I use the words *total commitment* because they're easier to get our minds around than the concept of "surrender." Total commitment says, "When I come to realize what God has done for me, who He is, and what He has prepared for me in this new life (that I cannot see), I eagerly abandon anything and everything to obtain this fabulous, rich, rewarding eternal life He is offering." It's not a matter of renunciation, but one of reevaluation.

> Total commitment is the channel through which God's best and biggest blessings flow.

So often the word *surrender* is associated with what we have to give up instead of what we get. During my first few years as a Christian, the words *surrender* and *total commitment* conjured up only concepts of sacrifice, renunciation, missing out, and losing what mattered most to me. I am convinced that most Christians "stall out" in the faith when the call to total commitment is received or viewed as something too high and too hard for them. Other well-meaning believers "stall out" or remain stuck because they have never been taught that total commitment is Christ's demand for all of His followers—without exception. In our efforts to be culturally relevant and make people feel comfortable in church, the preaching and teaching on this subject has been sadly omitted.

Surrender is not a dirty word. Total commitment is not reserved for spiritual superstars, pastors, missionaries, and those who are "more spiritual" than regular people like you and me. Total commitment is the channel through which God's best and biggest blessings flow. In the next chapter I'll help you rethink what it means to really surrender to God in order to give Him what He really wants so He can give you His very best!

IT'S YOUR MOVE—Become an ⊙12 Christian

God longs to speak personally to you. Take two minutes and slowly read through the TRUST ME questions and suggestions for spiritual growth. Now sit quietly for three minutes and ask God which of those questions or actions are pathways to grace that will strengthen and encourage you. Don't feel compelled to answer all the questions or do all that is suggested; listen to the Holy Spirit and follow His leading.

THINK—What is the main message of this chapter?

REFLECT—How have you viewed surrender or "total commitment" in the past?

UNDERSTAND—How do the stories of John and Sheila reframe your mental lens on surrender?

SURRENDER—Tell God all the things you fear you will lose if you *surrender* everything in total commitment to Him.

TAKE ACTION—Write out the definition of "total commitment" on a 3x5 card and read it every night before you go to bed.

MOTIVATION—What would God need to do to *convince* you that He desires to give you the very best for your life? (Romans 8:32; Psalm 37:4).

ENCOURAGE SOMEONE—Call or text the most committed Christian you know and thank them for their great example.

·

CHAPTER THREE

Do you believe God has your best in mind?

For my yoke is easy and my burden is light.[1]
—*Jesus of Nazareth*

In the last chapter, we were introduced to three case studies that challenge our warped view of total commitment or surrender. I don't think anybody read the last chapter feeling sorry for John, Sheila, or the man who found the treasure in the field. Yet as a pastor for twenty-five years, I can tell you, most people are deathly afraid of making a total commitment. Whether that total commitment is to another person in a lifelong vow of marriage, or whether it's a total commitment to God whereby we make a vow in our heart that all that we have and all that we are is surrendered to Him. As you may have noticed in the endnote on page 283, I took a page out of Jesus' teaching and made up a parable (the book—*Risk, Reason, and the Decision-Making Process*) that I hope helped you see surrender from God's perspective. So, don't go to amazon.com . . . you won't find this book there!

I think much of the teaching in the past on the subject of total commitment has emphasized the level of sacrifice and denial that is required rather than what Jesus pointed out as the level of joy and reward to be received. Don't get me wrong: it's not that there isn't sacrifice; but it's like giving up a necklace of cheap plastic pearls in order to receive a necklace of genuine, priceless ones.

How Total Commitment Really Works

So let's peel away our past perceptions and ask the question "What exactly is total commitment and how does it work?" First, let me give you a definition:

> *Total commitment is the alignment of one's motives, resources, priorities, and goals to fulfill a specific mission, accomplish a specific task or follow a specific person.*
>
> —*WEBSTER'S DICTIONARY*

So it's very clear that total commitment means absolute surrender. It means the alignment of your will, your mind, your emotions, your possessions, and your relationships around a person, goal, or cause. In Romans 12:1, God commands us to offer our bodies (ourselves) as a living sacrifice. He tells us that acceptable worship to Him begins with the act of surrender (or total commitment).

It's easy to hear those words and begin to emotionally withdraw and think that's too high a price, or that's something "I could never do." But I would argue that our initial emotional reaction to the call to total commitment is rooted in our warped view of God and our warped view of what total commitment actually is and what it is not. Total commitment is about being wise and smart, not necessarily being noble or virtuous. It's not so much about self-denial but about logic and common sense. It's not so much about what you lose; it's about what you gain.

It's not so much about what you lose; it's about what you gain.

Let me see if I can help you see it this way. On the facing page is a chart I created that looks at the issue of commitment or surrender through a positive and a negative lens. On the left side is a positive lens and on the right side is the negative lens. The positive lens looks at surrender (or total commitment) like the man who found the treasure in the field or the engineer who found the coins or the art teacher who found the painting—it's wise, logical, shrewd, and marked by a reevaluation of their present possessions in view of the greater reward. On the right side of the chart is the perspective of total commitment or surrender through the negative lens. This focuses on what we lose. Words like *sacrifice, self-denial, noble, martyr,* and *renunciation* characterize this negative view of total commitment.

POSITIVE VERSUS NEGATIVE	
Wise	Sacrifice
Logical	Self-Denial
Shrewd	Noble, Martyr
Reevaluation	Renunciation

Let me ask you, how do you tend to think of total commitment when it comes to your relationship with Christ? What is your greatest fear in surrendering all that you are and all that you have to Him? What pictures come to your mind when you think about making a total commitment to Christ that cause you to have fear or have second thoughts?

A Warped View of God

I know for me the issue was really rooted in a warped view of God. I assumed that if I made a total commitment, God would take away all my fun and keep me from the best things in life. Behind this false assumption was my complete misunderstanding of both God and the meaning of total commitment.

Somehow I got the idea that God was stingy, unkind, and looking to punish me for all the ways my life didn't measure up. I know these thoughts were rooted in bad theology and growing up apart from Christ; but even as I meet people from excellent Christian homes, I find that most Christ-followers don't really believe that God is good. Instead of a God who has a treasure awaiting His children and wants them to surrender—to make a total commitment so that He can give them the very best and biggest blessings—we live as though a total commitment to God would be a crushing blow to our personal dreams and future happiness.

When It Finally Clicked for Me

I remember when this came to light in my own life as I wrestled with this issue of surrender. Like many of you reading this book, I'd come to the point where I realized that God indeed demanded and required a total commitment of my life as His spiritual service of worship. But everything in me resisted the pull of His Spirit. One night after I'd lived two years both in the world and in the Word, a young couple invited me over for dinner to their home. They were brand-new Christians and had two small kids. As we ate dinner and talked about a relationship with the Lord, I saw a glimmer in their eye for each other that I longed to have someday with a wife of my own. I saw their love for their children, and despite their very humble financial status, they had a joy and warmth that was "*a treasure* if I've ever seen one."

It was a special night for reasons I can't quite explain, except I knew that what they had in their Christian life was what I was looking for in mine. It was *the treasure* of the life with God and with another person that no amount of money can buy. After a great homemade meal, followed by apple pie à la mode and a wonderful session of prayer around the kitchen table in their small farmhouse, I headed back to campus. As I was talking to God on my drive home and asking Him to give me what I saw in that young couple, I heard the Spirit explicitly say to my heart, "Chip, I want to give you the very best; but you won't let Me. As long as you maintain control of your life, you will always be destined to get *only what you can provide for your life*, not what I really want to give you."

The all-too-familiar battle about total commitment or surrender began to ensue. God's Spirit wooing me to decide once and for all that He could have complete control of my life, and my flesh arguing about all the sacrifice, denial, and loss that I would have to absorb if I made that commitment.

But as I drove onto the campus and slowly crept down the steep hill to my dorm room, the Spirit of God brought a verse to my mind that I'd recently memorized. It was Romans 8:32: "He that spared not His own Son [Jesus] but delivered Him up for us all, how will He not also along with Him [Jesus], *freely give us all things.*"

As my little Volkswagen made it to the bottom of the hill, the meaning of that verse began to resonate in my heart for the first time ever. It was as though God was saying, "Chip, if I love you enough to allow my Son to die in your place, how can you not believe that My plans for you are far better than anything you could come up with on your own?" It was in that moment that I realized the real issue in my relationship with God was far deeper than my struggle over surrender; the real issue was I didn't really believe that God really loved me or that He was good.

The real issue was I didn't really believe that God really loved me or that He was good.

IT'S YOUR MOVE—Become an ⊙12 Christian

What would happen in your life if you actually began to believe that God was really *for* you, that He understood your deepest desires and hidden fears? What if you saw God as a generous and kind friend who wanted to make sure you got the very best in life? What if God's call to surrender was more a pathway to unspeakable joy and lavish blessing than it was a measure of your spiritual fitness or level of sacrifice? How hard would it be to offer all that you are and all that you have to the One who says, "I have loved you with an everlasting love! You are the apple of My eye. I find holy pleasure in your happiness. I will quiet you with My love, and rejoice over you with singing"?

What would it look like to make a total commitment to that kind of God? How do we experience *spiritually* what John and Sheila experienced in the material world? How do we overcome our fears and begin to experience the life we've always wanted . . . whereby we receive God's biggest and best blessings through His divinely ordained channel, which He calls . . . surrender? Find out in the next chapter.

THINK—What part of this chapter spoke to you?

REFLECT—In one sentence, write down the top two barriers (fears) that keep you from making a total commitment to Jesus Christ.

UNDERSTAND—How does your view of God impact your ability to entrust your life to Him? How do you see God most days? Kind or demanding?

SURRENDER—God understands your fears. Sometimes we know (intellectually) what we need to do, but just can't seem to do it. Like the man who prayed "help my unbelief," ask Jesus to help you trust Him and see Him accurately.

TAKE ACTION—Write out Romans 8:32 on a 3x5 card and read it slowly every morning this week, asking God to help you believe what it says.

MOTIVATION—Listen to the message on the "Goodness of God" at **LivingontheEdge.org/r12** to recalibrate your view of Him.

ENCOURAGE SOMEONE—Share one thing God has done for you in the last few weeks with a friend. Ask them what He's done for them.

CHAPTER FOUR

What does a surrendered life look like?

I tell you the truth, unless a kernel of wheat falls
to the ground and dies, it remains only a single seed.
But if it dies, it produces many seeds.[1]
—*Jesus of Nazareth*

Most Christians are very confused about the meaning of surrender in their relationship to God. They simply don't know how it works. They think it's something noble and virtuous that only a few people "far more spiritual than them" are ever able to achieve.

But totally committed Christians are just ordinary people who are now experiencing God's biggest and best blessings. Moreover, they're not totally committed because they are super virtuous or spiritual. Rather, they are totally committed because they are wise, logical, and understand how life really works. But the question remains, what exactly does it look like to be totally committed? What does surrender look like in our relationship with God, and how does it work?

The Answer = Romans 12:1

Therefore I urge you brothers, in view of God's mercy, to offer your bodies as living sacrifices, holy and pleasing to God—this is your spiritual act of worship.

—ROMANS 12:1 NIV

I would like to make a couple of observations about this verse that I think will be very helpful. First, look at the structure of the passage. Notice that there is a command, a motivation, and a reason. The command is that you offer your body. The motivation is the mercy of God. And the reason is that it's the spiritual act of worship that God desires.

Second, I'd like you to understand the context of this passage. We're looking at Romans 12 and that means there are eleven chapters prior to this verse. In fact, I would highly encourage you to grab an iced tea or a cup of coffee and sit down sometime this week and quickly read the first eleven chapters of Romans in one sitting. It's one of the clearest explanations of all that God has done for us anywhere in the Bible. Below I've given you a brief outline of these first eleven chapters so that you can see that chapter 12 is in fact our response to the great things that God has done for you and me. The command to "offer your body" to God is not some way to gain His approval; it's our way of saying thank you to God in the light of all He has done for us.

ROMANS I–II: GOD'S MESSAGE OF GRACE

	CHAPTERS 1–3	CHAPTERS 4–5	CHAPTERS 6–8	CHAPTERS 9–11
TOPIC	Man's Problem	God's Solution	God's Provision	God's Faithfulness
THEOLOGY	Sin	Salvation	Sanctification	Sovereignty
STATE	Lost	Found	Empowered	Chosen
ACTION	Confession	Faith	Reckon	Praise

In this brief outline, chapters 1–3 identify the problem of all mankind—we have sinned and fallen short of God's glory. Then, in chapters 4 and 5, we see God's solution to our problem by sending Jesus,

God the Son, to die on the cross in our place to pay for our sins. We received this free gift of salvation by faith. In chapters 6–8, the Apostle Paul then describes how this new supernatural lifestyle is lived out. The Christian life that He describes in this section is not difficult, it's impossible. Only the Spirit of God dwelling in us has the ability to manifest the presence and the power of Christ in and through our mortal bodies. Finally, in chapters 9–11, we learn that God not only has a plan for our lives but has a future plan to fulfill all of His promises to the nation of Israel with regard to the throne of David and the land promised to Abraham.

What I want you to see, more than anything else, is that chapter 12 is looking back over the landscape of eleven chapters of God's great love and grace toward you. There's nothing that you or I can do to ever earn God's favor. But we are commanded to say thank you and to respond to God's grace in such a way that we get the very best from Him and He gets glory through us. That's the subject of Romans 12:1.

Now let's analyze Romans 12:1 together so we can understand what surrender or total commitment really looks like.

> *Therefore, I urge you, brothers, in view of God's mercy, to offer your bodies as living sacrifices, holy and pleasing to God—this is your spiritual act of worship.*
>
> —ROMANS 12:1 NIV

Check out what God commands in verse 1:

THE COMMAND = "OFFER YOUR BODIES AS LIVING SACRIFICES"
The command here is in a tense of the verb in Greek that tells us this offering of our bodies takes place at a specific point in time. This passage is not addressing how a person enters into a saving relationship with God; but how, after already knowing Him personally, we give God what He wants the most as our spiritual act of worship.

In my case, I'd been a Christian about two and a half years before I offered my body (life) in an act of total commitment and surrender to Christ. I was desperately struggling in my Christian life. My words said one thing, but my lifestyle communicated something totally contrary to being an authentic follower of Christ. I knew the truth but was not living it!

It was at this point that I found myself at Penn State University, where a parachurch organization put on a conference to teach college students how to take "next steps" in their spiritual growth. I took a two-hour seminar on the life of Abraham, in which we learned how God develops us in His school of faith.

I sat in the back of the room, examining my spiritual journey through the lens of the life of Abraham. It was clear that God valued faith far more than religious performance or even dutiful morality in Abraham's life. As the centrality of faith emerged in that seminar, God captured my attention when we made it to Genesis 22. There I heard the story of Abraham taking his only son, Isaac, up onto the mountain to sacrifice him to God. This boy had become the most important thing in Abraham's life—this twelve-year-old boy held all the promises that God had made to Abraham. Isaac was the promised son God had finally given to Abraham and now God was asking Abraham to literally give him back.

Abraham gets up early in obedience and takes the boy to the mountain, prepares an altar made out of rock, arranges sticks and wood for the fire, places Isaac up on the altar, and raises the knife, preparing to plunge it into his son's chest, when he hears a voice from heaven: "Abraham! Abraham! Do not lay a hand on the boy. Do not do anything to him. Now I know that you fear God, because you have not withheld from me your son, your only son" (Genesis 22:11–12, paraphrased).

Idols come in many forms. For Abraham, his son Isaac had become a point of affection that was en route to destroying his relationship with God. God demanded that Abraham surrender the most precious thing in his life—not to take it away from him, but to make sure he got the very best. As I sat in the back of that seminar, I realized that we all have Isaacs in our lives. For me, it was basketball and a beautiful girl I was dating at the time.

If God wanted to do anything in my life, it was fine with me as long as He didn't touch my two areas. Trusting Christ as my Savior and living out my faith in general was acceptable; but these two areas were "off-limits" to God's supervision or control. In reality, they were idols in my life that gave me my sense of identity and security.

In the back of that room I realized that I was at a crossroads in my life. Jesus was to be Lord "of all" or He was not Lord "at all." For the first time in my life I realized that far from withholding something good from me, surrender was God's channel through which His biggest and best blessings would flow into my life.

I finally realized that I needed to take "my Isaacs" up to the mountain and sacrifice them. It was a sober moment and not one that I took lightly. With empty palms in prayer in the back of that room I offered basketball, my future wife, my future career, and all that I was in a fresh, specific way as a living sacrifice to God. I knew the implications and I realized this offering of myself would need to be renewed day by day (as it says, a living sacrifice). I was taking the step of Lordship, which meant a radical departure from the norm—a life of holiness.

That day, in that room, on the campus of Penn State University, was the most pivotal moment in my Christian life. Despite many fears and much uncertainty I offered "all of me" to Him. Future decisions concerning every area of my life have been dramatically impacted since that day. I predecided to do "whatever God directed," trusting by faith He would always have my best in mind. Easy?! No way! Smart?! Yes! My journey from being a cultural Christian to an authentic follower of Jesus Christ began on that historic day in Pennsylvania.

It is this step that is sorely missing in the body of Christ today.

When I've had the opportunity to teach this passage on the radio and TV to nearly a million listeners, hundreds of people have e-mailed their responses telling us that they never understood what it meant to wholly surrender to Christ. Then they shared incredible stories of how taking this step brought about a transformation in their life—second only to their salvation. Like the merchant who sold all that he had to buy that one great pearl, or John the engineer who sold all that he had to get the twenty-two golden coins, so God calls you and me in gratitude to Him to offer our lives as a living and holy sacrifice. The question I have for you is: Have you ever done that?

THE MOTIVATION = "THE MERCY OF GOD"

If you're wondering, why should I surrender everything to God? Romans 12:1 says, "Therefore, I urge you brothers, in view of God's mercy, to offer your bodies as living sacrifices, holy and pleasing to God. You see, our motivation to surrender is not to earn anything. Our motivation is not to gain brownie points in heaven or stars on the great refrigerator in the sky; but it's a response to His mercy. It's grasping that our sins have been removed, that we are forgiven, loved, adopted, filled with the Spirit, and heaven-bound forever and ever. This is what motivates us to say thank you in the way that God requires. Saying thank you to God's grace and mercy is saying, "I believe that You are so loving and good that I will give You what You ask for . . . and that's me! All of me—holding nothing back."

THE REASON = "OUR SPIRITUAL ACT OF WORSHIP"

Why is it so important that I totally surrender to God? The last portion of this verse tells us. It is our spiritual act of worship. In other words, it's what God really wants. It's not your church attendance, your money, your rule keeping, your morality, or your religious activities: it's you.

God wants a relationship with you. He wants your heart. He wants to love you and be loved by you. He's not looking for little religious soldiers that will fulfill a cause for Him. He's looking for sons and daughters who so trust in His goodness and His love that they would with reckless abandon say, "All that I am and all that I have belongs to You. I love You, Lord!"

This is not primarily an emotional decision, but a logical one. The word that is translated as "spiritual," as in a spiritual act of worship, is an interesting one. The word *logizomai* literally means "that which is reasonable or logical." However, in the Greek translation of the Old Testament, this word came to be synonymous with offerings that priests made in the Temple—i.e., that which is a spiritual offering. As a result, translators are divided about how to capture the full meaning. The NIV translates the word as "spiritual" (to give weight to what God really wants), while the NASB translates it as "reasonable" (to give weight to the more literal meaning of the word—which is logical, smart, and well reasoned), i.e., surrender is logical and smart in light of what God has done for us in Christ.

The "Kingdom of God," as Jesus puts it, is about grasping what real life is all about and learning that the only way to gain it is by giving yourself away. "I tell you the truth, unless a kernel of wheat falls to the ground and dies, it remains only a single seed. But if it dies, it produces many seeds" (John 12:24). This is the normal expectation of Jesus for every believer. This step of Lordship is what opens the door to actually experiencing the power and presence of Jesus in a supernatural, transformational manner.

God has the freedom to do this only in those who are fully His.

In the words of G. K. Chesterton, "Christianity has not been tried and found wanting; it has been found and not tried."

You see, so much of what we have heard and been taught in years past misses or omits this Romans 12:1 call to surrender. Sincere yet uninformed Christians have been led to believe that the Christian life is little more than praying a prayer and attending some religious services. Authentic followers experience God's power and presence in supernatural, powerful ways because God has the freedom to do this only in those who are fully His.

IT'S YOUR MOVE—Become an ⊙12 Christian

Have you ever wondered what it would be like to experience God's power in this way? Do you want to know how to pull the trigger on a decision like this? How to you turn your intellectual belief into a living reality? That's in the next chapter. Stay with me.

THINK—What or who might be the "Isaac" in your life?

REFLECT—What do you fear the most about releasing your "Isaac" (an idol) and allowing Christ to be Lord of your life? What might be the underlying issues? Security? Significance? Control?

UNDERSTAND—What past experiences with family or other people make it hard for you to trust God? Could past abandonment, neglect, or divorce be unresolved issues making it hard to trust God?

SURRENDER—Why not take a moment right now to talk with God about what you are thinking, how you feel, and ask Him to direct your next steps.

TAKE ACTION—Write on a piece of paper or in your journal the people or things that might be an "Isaac" in your life. There is something powerful and clarifying about seeing in print deep issues that are sometimes difficult or painful to process.

MOTIVATION—Download the full-length audio message on *How to Give God What He Wants the Most* at **LivingontheEdge .org/r12.**

ENCOURAGE SOMEONE—Tell someone you care about to check out r12 online (LivingontheEdge.org/r12). Introduce them to God's dream for their life.

•

CHAPTER FIVE

Are you "all in"?

No one can serve two masters.
Either he will hate the one and love the other,
or he will be devoted to the one and despise the other.
You cannot serve both God and Money.[1]
—*Jesus of Nazareth*

Have you signed the check? The last thing I can remember my mother saying as I walked out the door was, "Whatever you do, don't lose that check!" In typical Chip fashion, I had waited till the last day to let my mom know that fees for school had to be paid that day or I would be left at home while the entire junior high went on a field trip. I can't even remember the exact amount, but it was more than just a few dollars. My mom didn't have any cash on hand, so she wrote me a check.

There was just one problem, I didn't know exactly how much the fee was going to be and I didn't know who to make it out to. The best quality about my mom is that she trusted me a lot—because as I look back, she did something that no parent should ever do. She signed the bottom of the check and left the rest completely blank. That meant if someone got this check or if I filled out my own name on the top, I could write out any amount and cash it for myself.

I know my mom wasn't worried about me, but when she signed that check, she made an open-ended commitment that all that she had in her bank account was available to whoever wrote their name on the top of the check and whatever amount was put on the line to the right.

Fortunately, I didn't lose the check, wrote the correct amount, and went on my field trip. But that story came to my mind when I thought about what it really looks like to surrender to Christ.

Yes, we've learned that our motivation is God's great love and mercy for us; and yes, we've come to understand that surrender is the channel through which God's biggest and best blessings flow; but how does it really work? How do you pull the trigger by faith in such a way that you become a living sacrifice, holy and acceptable to Him?

Unfortunately, I know a lot of Christians who spend the majority of their time "trying hard" to please God but never quite feeling like they measure up. Their Christian life is little more than multiple attempts of self-effort to gain God's approval. For others, the Christian life is more like fulfilling a duty and obligation on the weekend by attending a service and attempting to live in a moderately more moral way than the people around them. Both approaches completely miss God's heart and intent for His children.

Have You Signed the Check?

Regardless of what you may ever have thought, what God is looking for and wants most from you is *you*—all that you are and all that you have. I'd like you to picture your whole life as a blank check.

Imagine signing the bottom of the check, leaving the top part blank with regard to what God wants you to do, where He wants you to go, who He wants you to marry, or what career He would want you to pursue. And then you take that check in your mind's eye to the very throne room of God and slide it under the door as an act of worship to say to Him, "Lord, I want to commit all that I am and all that I have to You forever on this very day."

In many ways it's not unlike the marriage ceremony. It's a very specific commitment on a very special day that launches the relationship into an entirely new sphere of depth and intimacy. As I shared earlier,

I'd been a Christian a little over two years before I signed the bottom of the check and surrendered my life completely to Jesus Christ. But when I did, I began to experience the kind of Christian life that Jesus and the New Testament talk about. My question for you is simply this: Have you ever signed the bottom of the blank check and given it to God?

Have you ever humbly and honestly said to Him, "Lord, all that I am, and all that I have or ever hoped to have, is Yours. Use me as You think best?" If not, may I suggest that you set aside this book for a few moments and take that step right now? It is a decision that, when made in integrity, will change the course of your life.

You may be thinking, *I'm afraid. I can't do that right now. Why is it so important to surrender my life to Christ? Can't I just be a Christian on my own terms?* The answer is no, you can't be an authentic Christ-follower on your own terms for two reasons:

1. *Because God wants what's best for you.* Surrender is the *only* channel through which God's best and biggest blessings flow. He loves you, He's for you, He wants the very, very best for you!

2. *Your life either brings glory or disgrace to the name of Christ.* When we "accept Christ" and yet fail to follow Him and obey His commands, we misrepresent Him before a watching world. Many today reject Christianity not on the basis of logic or doctrine, but because of the inconsistency and hypocrisy of those who claim to be Christians. There is so much at stake!

So please, let me share with you the secret to surrender. I touched on it briefly in an earlier chapter, but I want to show you what keeps most Christians from surrendering their lives and missing God's good, acceptable, and perfect will.

The Secret to Surrender

When you surrender your life to Christ, you're declaring that you trust Him with your life and future. When I was wrestling with this decision and all the fears of "losing control of my life," God used Psalm 84:11 to seal the deal in my heart. I made it my Lordship passage and to this day I often quote it or pray it when I find myself struggling with obeying what God has called me to do.

> The LORD God is a sun and a shield. The LORD gives grace and glory, no good thing will He withhold from those who walk uprightly.

It's interesting that the first part of that passage talks about God's name and His character. The word LORD is God's covenant name, Yahweh, which means He is personal, all-powerful, and self-existent. The word translated "God" in this passage is Adonai, and it refers to the God of creation and provision. Imagine, the all-wise, all-powerful, self-existent, personal creator and sustainer of the universe is like a sun and a shield to those who have signed the blank check of surrender. It's a picture of God being an *unlimited resource* for you and the One who can provide *unlimited protection*, no matter how difficult your circumstances may be today or ten years from now.

The next line in the text reveals God's hopes and dreams for your life: "He gives grace and glory." Unlike what you've been led to believe or may secretly fear in your heart, God wants far better for you than you could ever imagine. He wants you to experience a rich and deep relationship with the opposite sex. He wants you in a job and a career that He especially designed you to thrive in and be fulfilled in doing. He wants you in a part of the country and in a local community of believers where you actually experience the supernatural love and belonging that you've always dreamed of. God is the CEO and Lord of the universe and His desire to be number one in your heart and life is the key to experiencing His grace and glory.

The final line of this verse is what has helped me more than any other sentence in the Bible to take steps of faith when I felt afraid: "no good thing will He withhold from those who walk uprightly." To follow Christ in obedience, especially when you don't feel like it, is the pathway to receive the very best from God. He will never withhold any good thing from you as you walk surrendered unto Him 24/7.

What Happened When I Signed the Check

Well, I told you the struggles and fears that I had in signing the bottom of the check, but I now am compelled to tell you about the goodness of God and the extent of His blessing when I was finally willing to trust His way instead of my own. My college basketball career was peppered with multiple injuries and multiple changes of coaches. As a result, it was anything but illustrious. When I finally made progress toward winning playing time, a major injury would sideline me (it happened two times!) for the rest of the year. On another occasion, right about the time I was starting to come into my own, we changed coaches three times within about four weeks. Needless to say, this dream of being a star basketball player for the glory of God was thwarted on multiple occasions.

By the middle of my senior year, I finally surrendered basketball to God and told Him that if I never played again, it would be okay with me. It's not something that I would ever choose, but if that's what He called me to do, I would be at least willing.

My senior year ended and I had a lot of peace as I played the final few games of the season. Toward the end of the year I received a letter from a group called Sports Ambassadors. They invited me to join other college basketball players from around the nation to travel overseas using basketball as a vehicle for evangelism. In the summers of 1976 and 1977, I found myself playing against Olympic teams in every country throughout South America. I had the privilege of playing with major college players from all over America who were committed Christians and at halftime we shared our faith. I played more games in one summer than I had in my entire college career, as we played one or two games daily against the best competition in all of South America.

In the winter of 1978, God opened yet another door to play basketball throughout Asia with an Australian team. We shared Christ and I had the time of my life! You see, the problem was never basketball itself; the problem was that basketball had become an idol in my heart and in my life.

In a similar fashion, I released my dating life to the Lord. It meant breaking up with a girl I loved very much but whose life vision and direction were clearly different from God's calling on my life. It hurt deeply and it took me nearly a year to get over the loss; but it was during that year of loneliness and hurt that I experienced an intimacy with Christ that I'd never known before. It also developed a new view and approach for building a relationship with a woman that was focused first and foremost on Jesus Christ. Allowing Him to direct that area of my life was painful, but it was one of the greatest decisions of my life.

My choices and your choices are always finite and limited—on our own, we will always choose second best for ourselves. There's only One being in all the earth who knows all things actual and possible and who cares so deeply for us that He is committed to giving us the very best; even when it means bringing pain or frustration into our lives to wean us from our idols.

Surrender is the secret to God's best. Surrender is the key to power. Surrender is the channel through which God's biggest blessings flow. Surrender is what allowed me to play basketball all around the world and then later meet and marry Theresa. *Surrender is the greatest need in the Body of Christ today.* Christians who by faith, in response to the glorious and amazing grace of God, say to Him at one specific point in their life, "All I am and all I have is Yours" can rest that God will "not withhold any good thing from them."

I'm All In!

As we close this critical chapter, I want to share one final word picture that has helped thousands of people get a handle on what surrender looks like in everyday life. One of the most popular new sports on television today is poker. I never quite thought of it as a sport, but when ESPN, the Travel Channel, and almost everyone else airs poker games multiple nights a week, I think it's safe to say that there must be a lot of interest. The game that seems to have captured America in recent years is called "Texas hold 'em." The biggest moment in Texas hold 'em comes when three little words are said: "I'm all in!"

At that point one player takes all the chips in front of him and pushes them to the center of the table. The drama now begins and the remaining players flip their cards faceup so everyone can see who has what and which cards will be needed to win the hand. The dealer then methodically and dramatically begins to turn over the last two or three cards to determine the winner. The person who has gone "all in" will either leave as a big winner or will be removed from the game, as every single chip that he or she possesses is at the center of the table.

Texas hold 'em demonstrates better than anything I know of what it means to surrender your life to Christ. The drama doesn't really get started and the action doesn't really begin until you say to God, "I'm all in!" It's when you take the chips of your family, your future, your money, your gifts, your dreams, and all your possessions and you push them to the middle of the table and you say, "Okay, Lord, you deal," that your life gets really exciting.

"I'm all in" is a contemporary picture of being a "living sacrifice, holy and pleasing to God." It's the moment a Christian transfers control from him- or herself to Jesus Christ. This transfer of trust called "surrender" or Lordship ignites a life of faith. It turns your life completely around as you ask, "Lord, what do you want me to do in . . . my work, my future, my marriage, my singleness, my spiritual gifts, with my money . . . to fulfill Your will and purposes in and through me?" A new adventure is launched as you seek to hear God's voice, wrestle with idols, experience His presence, and begin to witness vivid answers to prayer.

> This transfer of trust called "surrender" or Lordship ignites a life of faith.

God always has and always will look for men and women who say to Him, "I trust You so much, I'm all in. I want Your way not mine. I believe that Your plans and Your wisdom are better than mine. I am willing to live by faith!" When a man or woman takes this step, life is never the same.

IT'S YOUR MOVE—Become an **ρ12** Christian

As you think through this issue of surrender, let me encourage you to share your fears and doubts with a trusted and mature friend. Often we don't know what is really going on inside until we verbalize it in a safe environment. If that's not possible, pick up a cheap spiral notebook and journal your thoughts, fears, excitement, and doubts. You are about to begin a chapter of your life in Christ that will be filled with joy and power like you've never known; but it will be also a time of significant testing and spiritual opposition. Christians whose lives really make a difference threaten the enemy of our souls. In the next section, we'll learn who our enemy is and how to defeat him and his world system.

THINK—What is God saying to you in Romans 12:1?

REFLECT—Why does God want "all of you"? Why or why not is this a challenge for you?

UNDERSTAND—What or who is the best way for you to process your inner thoughts and feelings? Journal? Mentor? Long walk?

SURRENDER—Just do it! Sign the blank check. Tell God, "I'm all in" today.

TAKE ACTION—Write in your Bible the date you make your Romans 12:1 surrender to God and tell one other person.

MOTIVATION—Write out Psalm 84:11 on a 3x5 card and put it in your wallet or purse so you can read it each time you make a purchase this week.

ENCOURAGE SOMEONE—Share Psalm 84:11 with two people via e-mail, text, or letter this week.

B.I.O.
(BEFORE GOD DAILY, IN COMMUNITY WEEKLY, ON MISSION 24/7)

B.I.O. is the pathway to becoming an R12 disciple.

BEFORE GOD DAILY

Inherent in the idea of surrender is trust. You will not surrender to God unless you trust that He truly is good and knows best. Trust is developed out of relationship, and relationship is built on the investment of time. That's what coming *Before God Daily* is all about. Spending time in God's Word and in prayer is the key to a deep and intimate relationship with God. Developing the habit of setting aside time each day to *be* with God will revolutionize and turbocharge your spiritual growth.

But coming before God is also about living your entire life before Him. It means being conscious and aware of His presence. It means talking with Him throughout your day, asking for His help when you face temptation, expressing gratitude for His good gifts, and seeking His wisdom on decisions.

As you come before God in the weeks to come, intentionally look for examples in Scripture of surrender. As you look at people in Scripture, pay attention to some of the common barriers to surrender. Notice what God did as a result of people's willingness to surrender.

As you spend time in God's Word, search for verses and truths about God's character. Part of our journey in surrender is getting a clear and accurate view of God and learning that He really is good and benevolent and kind. Once that sinks in, surrender feels more like an exciting adventure than a scary demand.

IN COMMUNITY WEEKLY

As was discussed in this section, surrender is a point-in-time decision when you once and for all declare Jesus as the rightful King and Lord of your whole life. But it is an ongoing challenge to stay surrendered. It is easy for us to drift into self-seeking. There are a thousand subtle seductions that pull at us to live for ourselves and take back control from God.

One of the greatest threats to surrender is that of wearing masks. Masks project the image that we have it all together, that life is dialed-in. That leads to a life of duplicity, propping up an image publicly that is different from who I really am privately.

That's why authentic community is so important in your life. We all need friends who know the "real" us and will help us stay surrendered to God. But it will require you to take off your mask, open up your life, and invite a few trusted friends to help you in your journey of surrender.

So, if you aren't in a small group, consider joining one. Get intentional about pursuing the kind of relationships that will speak truth into your life and help you stay surrendered.

ON MISSION 24/7

Surrender is crucial to being on mission. 2 Corinthians 5 gives us a good word picture to understand the connection between being surrendered and being on mission. When Paul is declaring that God has given us the ministry of reconciliation, he says that we are "Christ's ambassadors, as though God were making his appeal through us." An ambassador was a citizen of another land and was subject to his king. The ambassador served at the king's discretion and carried out the purposes of his king.

What a great picture of surrender. As you move toward becoming an R12 disciple, begin to picture yourself as an ambassador. You are a citizen of a different country (heaven) and this world is not your home. Your assignment on this planet is not to carry out your own agenda, but rather to carry out the purposes of your king. And remember that you have been given the "ministry of reconciliation." Part of your assignment is help those around you become friends with your king.

.

How to Get God's Best for Your Life

SEPARATE FROM THE WORLD'S VALUES
ROMANS 12:2

The greatness of God rouses fear within us,
but His goodness encourages us not to be afraid of Him.
To fear and not be afraid—that is the paradox of faith.[1]
—*A. W. Tozer*

•

CHAPTER SIX

Are you getting God's best?

Then he said to them all: "If anyone would come after me,
he must deny himself and take up his cross daily and follow me.
For whoever wants to save his life will lose it,
but whoever loses his life for me will save it." [2]
—*Jesus of Nazareth*

I hope and pray that you finished the last chapter on surrender by taking that step of saying "I'm all in" with God. It's not only what God wants most from you; it is the secret to getting the *very best* from Him.

How Do You Get the Very Best from God?

In this section, we'll consider this question by studying Romans 12:2:

Do not conform any longer to the pattern of this world, but be transformed by the renewing of your mind. Then you will be able to test and approve what God's will is—his good, pleasing and perfect will.

You have probably heard this verse before, as it is often quoted, but when I hear it, the *emphasis* is usually on the first eleven words, *"Do not conform any longer to the pattern of this world."* Those are very important words and we will study them carefully, but it's the last nineteen words that so often get overlooked: *"Then you will be able to test and approve what God's will is—his good, pleasing and perfect will."*

For just a minute, forget the first part of this passage. Can you imagine that there is something we can actually do that God promises will allow us to "test and approve" (the idea is to fully and completely experience) how good, pleasing, and perfect His will is for our lives? Think about that! Whoa! God wants you to experience His good and pleasing will in your marriage, your job, and your future. He even wants you to experience His perfect will in a difficult situation as you learn to wait, learn, and see God's wisdom and grace sustain you.

All that to say: God wants to give you the very best. I didn't say the easiest, and don't confuse "the best" with how you define it. But the Creator of the universe knows your name, sees your heart, knows your pain, and longs to pour out His good, acceptable, and perfect will into every area of your life and relationships.

Sadly, most Christians don't experience God's best. Most Christians get seduced and conned into believing lies that keep them conformed to this world and they miss out on all the wonderful things God wants to give them.

There's a Real Battle to Get God's Best

I shared about my early years as a Christian in chapter one, when I was torn between two worlds. My life was a mess. Bible study and bars. Sacred moments with God in the morning and sexual fantasies at night.

I honestly wondered if I would ever escape from that "caught in the middle" going-nowhere season of my life. I tried to change. I promised God repeatedly that I would change and I sincerely wanted to change, but I didn't know how. I didn't understand the first part of Romans 12:2. I didn't have any idea what the world system was or how it worked.

I didn't know what it meant to renew my mind, let alone why I was stuck! How about you? How are you doing? What is holding you back?

I wish my experience was atypical, but the true reality is about nine out of ten Christians have been "tripped up" somewhere along the way that keeps them from experiencing those last nineteen words of Romans 12:2. It breaks my heart as I read hundreds of e-mails from sincere believers who are stuck and often don't know how to move forward. For example, a young woman writes:

> *Thank you for your broadcast this morning from the series "Becoming a Romans 12 Christian." I was saved when I was thirteen but have gone through a lot of hard times throughout college and my relationship with God has been up and down. Lately I've been feeling so lethargic and distant from God. I woke up this morning and asked myself the question, "If I die today, what would people say about me?" And I honestly I didn't think they would use the words* Christian *or* messenger for God *as one of my first descriptions . . . or even one at all.*
>
> It was then that I happened to turn on your program while washing dishes and it was really a blessing to me. I've been struggling so much with alcoholism and sexual immorality, and Today I decided to give all of myself to God and to completely surrender myself to Him. So thank you and God bless you.

This woman has taken the first step—surrender, but that *point in time* must be followed by a *spiritual process* that we will learn in Romans 12:2 if lasting transformation is to occur. Just yesterday, I received an e-mail entitled "HELP!" In this e-mail a man describes taking some very specific steps last January that caused a dramatic change in his life after only a few

Today I decided to give all of myself to God and to completely surrender myself to Him.

months. Further along in his e-mail, he describes his gradual slippage and the deception that plunged him headlong into the destructive life-style patterns of his past.

My point: You and I are in a battle. We all struggle. We will all have missteps and failures on our journey; but it is God's desire *for you* to experience His good, pleasing, and perfect will.

The battle will change as you continue to mature, but real transformation is possible. I still struggle at times with my thought life and I am very susceptible to visual messages, so I have had to be very intentional about what I watch or where I let my eyes go. I have battled workaholism, pleasing people, and self-righteousness in my journey. I rejoice at God's work in my life, but I still have daily temptations and challenges as the world's values bombard me. But I will also tell you that deep, lasting, significant change has occurred in my motives, speech, behavior, and relationships, which have been deeper and better than I ever imagined. God's good and perfect will is sweet.

That life is available and waiting for you. Those last nineteen words can describe your life when you learn by faith to put into practice the first twenty words of Romans 12:2. In the next four chapters, we will continue our journey together in order to do exactly that—learn how to practically experience His good, pleasing, and perfect will in *your* life.

IT'S YOUR MOVE—Become an **e12** Christian

God longs to speak personally to you. Take two minutes and slowly read through the TRUST ME questions and suggestions for spiritual growth. Now sit quietly for three minutes and ask God which of those questions or actions are pathways to grace that will strengthen and encourage you. Don't feel compelled to answer all the questions or do all that is suggested; listen to the Holy Spirit and follow His leading.

THINK—Read Romans 12:2 over slowly with special focus on the last nineteen words.

REFLECT—What comes to your mind when you think about doing God's will? Does your mind gravitate to words like *difficult, painful, distasteful;* or do you see His will as good, well pleasing, and custom made for your benefit and joy? Why?

UNDERSTAND—How and where have you struggled the most in your journey with Christ? What habits, sins, or setbacks seem to thwart your relationship with Christ?

SURRENDER—Ask God to begin opening your eyes and your heart to what His good and pleasing will is for your life.

TAKE ACTION—Watch "How to Get God's Best for Your Life"—a twelve-minute video on Romans 12:2. **Go to LivingontheEdge.org/r12.**

MOTIVATION—Write out this prayer on a 3x5 card or in your own personalized version and tape it on your mirror:

Father, help me not to let this world squeeze me into its mold,
but transform me from the inside out as I meditate
and apply Your Word to my life.

ENCOURAGE SOMEONE—Jot a brief note to someone who knows Christ, but is not walking with Him. Just let them know you care and are praying for them today.

•

CHAPTER SEVEN

Why is the Christian life so difficult?

What good is it for a man to gain the whole world,
and yet lose or forfeit his very self?[i]
—Jesus of Nazareth

Most Christians have no idea why living the Christian life is so difficult. In the last chapter we discussed the battle that every believer engages in on a daily basis. But if you don't understand the battle, the enemy that you face, and where the battle is fought, you are destined to spiritual failure, frustration, and eventually despair. I believe most Christians want to follow Christ. There's just one problem: we live in a toxic environment to our spiritual health. This toxic environment involves a who, a where, and a what.

Know Your Enemy

The who is Satan. He is the architect of this evil, toxic environment. His original name was Lucifer. He was the most beautiful and intelligent of all the beings God created. The Bible tells us that Satan's sin centered on his pride and overwhelming beauty. This led to his attempt to usurp God as the ruler and king of the universe. This story is outlined in Isaiah 14 and Ezekiel 28. Satan led one third of the angels in a spiritual rebellion against God. He is the author of evil, and those angels who accompanied his rebellion are now referred to in Scripture as "demons," "principalities," and "powers of darkness."

Satan's goal was clearly defined by Jesus when He said, "The thief comes only to steal and kill and destroy" (John 10:10). It is critical for you to understand as a follower of Christ that you have a spiritual enemy. As the Apostle Paul warns us in Ephesians:

> *For our struggle is not against flesh and blood, but against the rulers, against the authorities, against the powers of this dark world and against the spiritual forces of evil in the heavenly realms.*
>
> —EPHESIANS 6:12

You are in a spiritual battle and the stakes are very high. You have an enemy whose goal is to destroy your life, your relationships, and your testimony for Jesus Christ.

Recognize What the World Tells You Every Day

But you need to understand more than simply who your enemy is; you must understand where and how he operates. The where of Satan's operation is called "the world," or what is commonly referred to as the world's system. The Greek word *a-eon* (used in Romans 12:2) refers not to the physical world that you see, but to a spiritual world system. This world system is designed to woo your heart away from God, destroy your relationships with others, and lead you into sin that brings condemnation to your heart and broken fellowship with your heavenly Father.

This world system (cosmos) is defined in Scripture as the *lust of the flesh*, the *lust of the eyes*, and the *pride of life* (1 John 2:15–17). In the next chapter we will unpack exactly what the world system is and how it seeks to warp your thinking, blind your eyes, and seduce your soul. But before we investigate the world system, you need to understand not only the who (Satan) and the where (the world system) of your spiritual battle, but also the what.

Recognize the Ongoing Battle within You

The what is something the Bible calls "the flesh" or what some translations refer to as our "old self" or "old man." Many Christians are confused and frustrated to discover that after coming to know Christ, they still struggle with old sins and habitual sin patterns. If we are forgiven and are new creations in Christ, why do we still struggle and fall back into some of our old patterns of life? More important, what can we do about it? To answer these questions we need to get a clear understanding of what actually occurred when we trusted Christ and what obstacles still remain.

When you placed your faith in Jesus Christ as your personal Savior, a number of significant things happened in your life:

- Your sins were immediately forgiven.
- You received the imputed righteousness of Jesus Christ.
- You were placed in God's family.
- You were taken out of the kingdom of darkness and placed into the Kingdom of Light.
- The Holy Spirit entered your physical body.
- You became a son or daughter of the living God, solely by the grace God provided for you through the work of Jesus Christ on the cross and His resurrection.

This eternal, spiritual transaction occurred when you heard the good news of the Gospel of Jesus Christ and by faith received the gift of salvation. Scripture describes this as being "born again" or being born "from above." The Apostle Paul describes this transaction as a work of redemption whereby you were purchased for God by the blood of Christ (1 Corinthians, 6:19–20). As a result, you presently possess four magnificent gifts from God:

- You are now God's son or daughter.
- You have peace with God.
- The Holy Spirit sealed you for all eternity and lives within you.
- The penalty of sin was forgiven and the power of sin was broken.

What many believers do not understand is that every believer still has the capacity to sin. Although our sins are forgiven and we now have the power to overcome temptation, we will forever struggle with sin because we still have what the Bible calls "the flesh." This is the capacity that dwells within all God's children that is bent toward the old life, the old ways, and the desire to live apart from God's rule in our life. This is the what I referred to earlier. The Apostle Paul summarizes this battle in Galatians 5:17:

Every believer still has the capacity to sin.

> For the flesh sets its desire against the Spirit, and the Spirit against the flesh; for these are in opposition to one another, so that you may not do the things that you please.

These two forces are constantly fighting each other, and your choices are never free from this conflict. So you see, authentic followers of Christ follow Him in the midst of a hostile and toxic environment. Satan is a liar and deceiver who uses the world system that he has created to tempt God's children according to the desires of their flesh to bring about their destruction. Unfortunately, most Christians do not understand the battle they are fighting, the enemy that they face, or the means God has provided to overcome the temptations and deception of this present world system. As a result, most Christians, though sincere, find themselves living a life of duplicity and compromise.

After multiple efforts to seek to obey the commands of the New Testament and emulate the life of Jesus, most believers find themselves frustrated and defeated. Trying hard to do what's right and going to religious activities are ineffective means of overcoming temptation and the deceptive lies of the world system. After pastoring for twenty-five years, I cannot tell you how typical it is to encounter well-meaning Christ-followers who live with an inner life characterized by guilt and shame. After years of self-effort and spiritual failure, most retain a superficial acknowledgment of faith in Jesus while their lifestyle demonstrates very little difference from that of their non-Christian friends. This problem is not new; it was just as prevalent in the early church. That's why God provides the answer to this dilemma in Romans 12:2:

> Two forces are constantly fighting each other, and your choices are never free from this conflict.

Do not conform any longer to the pattern of this world, but be transformed by the renewing of your mind. Then you will be able to test and approve what God's will is—his good, pleasing and perfect will.

In Romans 12:1, we learned how to give God what He wants the most—the surrendering of ourselves to Him. This commitment occurs after salvation (for most) at a specific point in time in our lives. We declare Jesus as Lord of all we are and all that we have. This defining Lordship event is then followed by a process. This process is outlined in Romans 12:2. Notice that this process is characterized by two commands and a purpose clause:

Two Commands and a Purpose

NEGATIVE COMMAND: "DO NOT BE CONFORMED TO THE PATTERN OF THIS WORLD . . ."

"Do not be conformed"

- Passive voice
- Imperative
- Present tense

Expanded Translation: "Stop allowing yourselves to be molded by the *influences* and *pressures* of this present world system."

POSITIVE COMMAND: ". . . BUT BE TRANSFORMED BY THE RENEWING OF YOUR MIND."

"Be transformed"

- Passive voice
- Imperative
- Present tense

Expanded Translation: "But allow God to completely change your *inward thinking* and *outward behavior* by cooperating wholeheartedly moment by moment with the Spirit's renewing process."

PURPOSE CLAUSE: "THEN YOU WILL BE ABLE TO TEST AND APPROVE WHAT GOD'S WILL IS—HIS GOOD, PLEASING AND PERFECT WILL."

Expanded Translation: "So that our lives (our very lifestyles 24/7) will experience and demonstrate what God's will really is—that which is good, acceptable, and perfect."

The first command is negative, "Do not conform any longer to the pattern of this world." The second command is positive, "but be transformed (changed from the inside out) by the renewing of your mind." The purpose clause is why God wants us to declare war on the lies of this present world's values and why He wants our minds renewed in accordance with His Word, "So that our lives (our very lifestyles 24/7) will experience and demonstrate what His will really is—that which is good, acceptable, and perfect."

I cannot describe to you the heartbreak I've witnessed over the years at the sight of fellow Christians who are trapped in addictions and held captive by sinful lifestyle patterns. They have been robbed of their joy, lost jobs, and fractured families, and become prisoners of their own passions. They do not understand how Satan uses the world system to influence their thinking in ways that have ruined relationships and broken intimacy with God. If only they understood how to apply Romans 12:2, their lives would be completely different. So let's take a closer look at this text.

The verb in "Do not be conformed" is in the passive voice—a use of the verb that denotes the subject is receiving the action—the world is actively molding us. The sentence also contains an imperative—which means it is a command, a prohibition, it has to do with our will. Finally, this verb is in the present tense—that which is being forbidden was actually happening right then in the church. The above lesson in grammar provides some interesting results. My expanded translation of this text reflects these grammatical insights:

Stop allowing yourselves to be molded by the influences and pressures of this present world we live in. Stop allowing Satan to dupe you, con you, use you, trick you, promise you life and love and power through a seductive world system that will only deliver disappointment, defeat, depression, and make you a slave to sin.

How long will we as followers of Christ keep buying the lie that sex, salary, and status will really make us a "somebody"? When will you pull back the veil of deception and realize that pleasure, possessions, and position apart from God will never satisfy the deepest needs of your souls?

I shared in the last chapter my struggle and my journey in this area. Although I was a genuine child of God, my mind was dominated by lust. My thinking and behavior were rooted in a false belief that sexual gratification and popularity as a star performer would bring lasting happiness and fulfillment. I worshipped the idol of myself and used the opposite sex as a means of self-gratification rather than as an opportunity for genuine love and deep relationship. In addition, basketball was far more than a game to be played in college; it was my attempt to gain status in the eyes of others and prove by my performance that I was important and worthy of attention. I poured my life into how I looked, how I performed, whom I could impress, and how I could get what I wanted.

My lips and my life told two very different stories—and in my most honest moments the guilt and duplicity was crushing. I had to keep moving fast and pushing down the Spirit's conviction as I lived this double life. Internally I was miserable, and externally I was misrepresenting and tarnishing the name of the One who gave up His life on the cross for me. Looking back, it's all very clear. But at the time I really didn't know why the Christian life was so hard and why what began as an amazing and joy-filled adventure had turned into an ugly battle that I was losing most the time.

IT'S YOUR MOVE—Become an e12 Christian

How about you? How are you doing in the battle? What kind of duplicity do you see in your life? Have you ever paused to consider that you may be missing out on God's best for your life? Do you want to change? Would you like to understand what exactly this world system is and why it is so powerful in stealing your heart and affections from your Lord?

Well, that's what's ahead. In the next chapter we will explore what exactly this "world system" is and how it works day in and day out in your life and mine.

THINK—What new insight did you gain from this chapter?

REFLECT—Why is the Christian life so difficult? What specific strategies does the enemy use in this world system that tempt you the most?

UNDERSTAND—How do you currently combat the influences of the "world's values" in your life? What is working? What's not?

SURRENDER—Share honestly with God where you struggle the most in your life. Then sit quietly and listen after asking God to reveal *anyone* or *anything* that is currently a hindrance to your relationship with Christ.

TAKE ACTION—Address whatever God reveals to you in prayer as you listen. Ask Him for forgiveness and claim 1 John 1:9.

MOTIVATION—Listen to the full-length audio message on "How to Get God's Best for Your Life" on Romans 12:2 at **Living ontheEdge.org/r12.**

ENCOURAGE SOMEONE—Invite someone who is really struggling spiritually to your home for dinner, or to a Bible study, or for coffee just to "catch up."

.

CHAPTER EIGHT

Are you a faithful lover?

*Then Jesus was led by the Spirit into the desert
to be tempted by the devil. After fasting forty days and forty nights,
he was hungry. The tempter came to him and said,
"If you are the Son of God, tell these stones to become bread."* [1]
—*The Temptation of Jesus*

David (not his real name) was absolutely shaken. His face was white as he recounted the story of the last twenty-four hours. Tears rolled down his cheeks as he shared with me that he had learned that his wife had been unfaithful. The night before, a local police officer spotted a van in a remote area with the lights out. His investigation of the situation revealed David's wife having sex with another man in the back of his van. His emotions were all over the map; from anger to embarrassment to outright expressions of denial. You deal with a lot of issues as a pastor of a local church, but few compare to the pain and devastation that occurs when one marriage partner learns that their spouse has committed adultery.

No Other Lovers!

I share that story in hopes that you catch the depth of emotion and the level of pain and rejection that occurs in someone's heart when they are betrayed in a relationship. Affairs destroy relationships. Affairs break trust. No relationship can be sustained when one member of the relationship pretends to be devoted to their mate while secretly living a double life. We can tolerate any number of imperfections in our spouses; but there is one area where we draw a line in the sand . . . "No Other Lovers!"

In Romans 12, this is essentially God's position with us. "Do not be conformed any longer to the pattern of this world . . ." is God declaring that for the health of our relationship with Him, He tolerates "No Other Lovers!" "This world" or cosmos does not refer to the physical world but to a worldview or world system whose architect is Satan. When God commands us "not to be conformed" or allow the world's values to squeeze us into its mold, He is giving us a command concerning spiritual fidelity. Many times in the Old Testament God spoke of His people as spiritual adulterers who had turned away from Him to worship idols. In this passage the Apostle Paul makes the same point with one phrase, *the world,* loaded with meaning for his first-century readers and us as well.

How God Defines "the World"

What exactly is "the world"? What does it consist of? How does it have the power to mold or influence our lives? How do sincere Christ-followers get seduced by "the world" and its values and commit spiritual adultery? How can we avoid the devastating personal and relational consequences of being seduced by the world? In this chapter we will explore the answer to these questions.

Sometimes the best commentary on Scripture is Scripture itself. In other words, a phrase like *the world* is used elsewhere in the Bible in a manner that specifically explains the meaning of the phrase. In 1 John 2:15–17, we have that passage:

Do not love the world nor the things in the world. If anyone loves the world, the love of the Father is not in him. For all that is in the world, the lust of the flesh and the lust of the eyes and the boastful pride of life, is not from the Father, but is from the world. The world is passing away, and also its lusts; but the one who does the will of God lives forever.

Notice how many times the word *love* is used in these three verses. I've bolded them to help you see them quickly. This passage is about love, it's about relationship. I've also underlined the phrase *the world* to help you see that the subject of this passage is about a competition for our love—"the world" and all it offers versus God and all He offers. "All that is in the world" is followed by three very specific things that make up the world system or world's values. They are the lust of the flesh, the lust of the eyes, and the pride of life. Since these are not terms that we tend to use in everyday conversation, let me break it down for you:

- The lust of the flesh = the passion "to feel"—this is hedonism.
- The lust of the eyes = the passion "to have"—this is materialism.
- The pride of life = the passion "to be"—this is egotism and self-centeredness.[2]

The world's system and its values are clearly expressed in these three passions. They are the supercharged desires we have for pleasure, possessions, and position that promise significance, security, and happiness. The message behind every commercial and nearly all advertisements is rooted in tapping into one of these desires. The lust of the flesh is about sex. It's about gratifying our needs with that which will bring sensual pleasure with an ever-insatiable need for more. The lust of the eyes is about salary and the power and control that money can bring. The pride of life is about status and superiority. It's about having or achieving those outward symbols that communicate our value, status, and importance.

A Good Thing in a Bad Way

Please carefully note that each of these worldly values is rooted in legitimate needs and longings that God has given us as human beings. The need for food, the desire for sex, the importance of recreation and pleasure are all important and not to be considered evil. But the world's system seeks to give you a good thing in a bad way or at a bad time.

For example, sex is a gift created by God for two people who are married. It is intended for pleasure, for procreation, and as a means to passionately communicate one's love and commitment to one's mate. But that same legitimate desire for sex, when taken outside the marital bounds, becomes an end in itself. We live in an absolutely sex-saturated society. Whether it is magazines at the checkout counter at the grocery store, the products you "need" to look and feel sexy, or annoying "pop-ups" on your computer inviting you to XXX Web sites—sex dominates the thinking, attitudes, and behaviors in this world. Christians are certainly not immune to the pulls and tugs of the sexual messages that bombard you hundreds of times a day. God's warning is that these false views of sexuality with their promises of fulfillment are in direct competition for your heart and mind.

In like manner, there's certainly nothing wrong with owning and possessing things we need to live. It's not wrong to own a home or car or have money in the bank. But the lust of the eyes is that passion to possess more, and bigger, and better in an attempt to prove our worth, provide security, and impress those around us.

The lust of the eyes is what produces workaholics and shopaholics. It is this same worldly lust that accounts for the massive personal debt and financial pressure the majority of Christians live under daily. These are all indicators that our hearts have been seduced by another lover—the other god—money. How many people (beginning with ourselves) do you know who work insane hours to buy things they do not need, to impress people they don't know, to the detriment of their health, their family, and their spiritual growth?

The third seducer of the world's system is the pride of life. It's the passion "to be"—to be significant, important, famous, out front, treated special, and viewed as better than others. It's having your ego and your needs at the center of the universe. This passion to be number one, get ahead, beat the competition, show the world your superiority comes out in everything from youth sports to the highest offices in the land.

People lie, cheat, backstab, bribe, and do almost anything to gain a position of influence, power, or popularity. Whether it's "sharing your dirty laundry" on a reality TV show or seeking to buy a senatorial seat in the government, our unbridled passion for our own glory is devastating to a relationship with Jesus Christ.

God has spoken in no uncertain terms: "I am the LORD, that is My name; I will not give My glory to another, nor My praise to graven images" (Isaiah 42:8). So often we begin with pure motives in our work, families, ministries, sports, and relationships only to gradually allow them over time to become "all about us." That's how the world system works on people like you and me.

Sex, Salary, and Status . . . at Your Doorstep

I've heard these three worldly values described in a number of ways. But what I don't want you to miss as you look at the chart on the following page is that these supercharged passions are at work daily in the world through TV, movies, advertisements, fashions, magazines, and popular culture. They are strategically designed to seduce your heart away from Christ. Satan has created a set of values in this fallen world that appeal to your flesh and tempt you to meet legitimate needs and longings to feel and to have and to be . . . totally apart from God. As you read over the chart, ask the Holy Spirit to show you which of the three worldly values you are most vulnerable to.

	THE WORLD'S PASSIONS		THE WORLD'S TEMPTATIONS	
"TO FEEL"	Sex	Pleasure	Girls/Guys	Food
"TO HAVE"	Salary	Possessions	Gold	Fortune
"TO BE"	Status	Position	Glory	Fame

Fifty years ago Christians regularly heard multiple sermons about the evils of some of the things listed above. In our efforts to shake off the "funcy" of the old fundamentalist movement and become relevant to "the culture," it appears we have fallen into it. The emphasis of fundamentalism often threw out "the baby with the bathwater" by condemning the role of God-ordained pleasure, the beauty of sexual intimacy, and the healthy stewardship and enjoyment of possessions. In reaction to a Christianity that was high on "rules" and low on "fun," I fear we have become a generation of Christians convinced that sex, salary, and status are the real keys to a life of fulfillment and happiness.

The average believer, according to recent research, does not live in an appreciably different way from those outside of Christ. The culture's promises of red-hot sex, a big home, a great job, and upward mobility have resulted in unprecedented divorce, financial collapse, disenfranchised children, and widespread depression among many who claim the name of Christ. The church of the twenty-first century is weak and worldly.

Consider how the views of Christians don't measure up to traditional Christianity. Kinnaman and Lyons share the following data in their book *unChristian*. Their study examined born-again busters (23–41) with born-again older adults (42+).

Those who find the following morally acceptable:

AGE	23–41	42+
• Cohabitation	59%	33%
• Gambling	58%	38%
• Sexual thoughts or fantasies about someone	57%	35%
• Sex outside of marriage	44%	23%
• Looking at pornography	33%	19%
• Having an abortion	32%	27%
• Homosexual behavior	28%	13%

A percentage of Christians simply hold views that are contrary to Scripture. And you can tell from how younger Christians view biblical values that the situation isn't getting better. These are not meant to be hard words of condemnation, but sad and sober facts.[3]

Who Do You Really Love?

Read slowly and carefully with me the command in 1 John 2:15, "Do not love the world [the world's values as a means to fulfill the deepest longings in your heart] nor the things of the world." Why? "If anyone loves the world the love of the Father is not in him." Do you realize what this means? Can you even remotely grasp what it would be like to love someone so much that you would leave all that you have, suffer unjustly for them, be ridiculed, mocked, and rejected by those you love, and then voluntarily die in their place only to be rejected and betrayed by them as you watch them run into the arms of another lover (the world—whose architect and designer is Satan himself).

If you think, by chance, I'm pushing the envelope a bit on this point, consider what Jesus' half brother James writes when discussing an authentic follower's relationship with this present world's system:

> *You adulterous people, don't you know that* friendship with the world *is hatred toward God? Anyone who chooses to be a* friend of the world *becomes an enemy of God. Or do you think scripture says without reason that the spirit he caused to live in us envies intensely?*
>
> —JAMES 4:4–5

At times when I read this passage I literally weep over the state of the church. At other times I read this passage and look inside my own heart, and it makes me very sad. You see, the world system operates everywhere. You can be a proud pastor doing the work of God, yet your "lust of the eyes" can be a bigger ministry rather than a bigger house or a bigger company. "Being worldly" (as they used to call in the olden days) is not primarily about external behaviors and a list of rules of what one can or cannot do. At the heart of "worldliness" is who you love and who you trust to meet the deepest needs of your life. When I look at it that way, I get less preoccupied with some of the external arguments about what's acceptable or not acceptable and a lot more focused on my love relationship with Jesus. Where are you at? How are you doing? Has the world system seduced your heart? How do you change? What's the answer?

At the heart of "worldliness" is who you love and who you trust to meet the deepest needs of your life.

I am personally convinced that much of our worldliness is a total misunderstanding of the real issue. There are far too many people who are stuck in cycles of sin that they repeat over and over again because they think the issue is their actual behavior. Behavior is almost always only the symptom. The real issue is far deeper.

If we would begin to feel deeply sad about running into the arms of another lover and comprehend how deeply this grieves our God who loves us and longs to give us the best, I think we would see a lot more Christians living like Christians.

I'm amazed that even in our sin we figure a way to make it "about us." My sin, my problem, my behavior, my addiction, my struggles, my difficult background, are all words and phrases that focus on us. "Love not the world, neither the things that are in the world—the lust of the flesh, the lust of the eyes, and the pride of life." Why? Because when we do, we become spiritual adulterers. We break trust. We destroy ourselves and others. But most of all, when we love the world, we break fellowship with our heavenly Father and receive consequences for our sin instead of the transformation of our soul.

IT'S YOUR MOVE—Become an ⊘12 Christian

So how does it work? How do you experience victory over these world's values? How can you become spiritually pure without becoming culturally irrelevant? How do you break free if you are stuck in some stronghold of sin? Well, that's what we'll talk about in the next chapter.

THINK—Where has God spoken to you in this chapter? Where's the single biggest issue that surfaced in your life?

REFLECT—How does seeing "the world" as a seductress change its appeal? How does reframing sin as a "relational issue" versus "breaking the rule" make you feel about times when you sin?

UNDERSTAND—Where are you most vulnerable to the world's deception?

- Lust of the eyes
- Lust of the flesh
- Pride of life

SURRENDER—Ask God to give you the courage to come out of your denial and rationalizations and be ruthlessly honest with yourself and Him. Be real, own your stuff, repent, and receive God's forgiveness.

TAKE ACTION—Do a three-, five-, or seven-day media fast. Break the supply lines of TV, movies, and all non-work-related computer activities . . . and watch what happens. (Romans 13:14.)

MOTIVATION—Listen or read "How to Break Out of a Destructive Lifestyle" from the Miracle of Life Change series at **LivingontheEdge.org/r12.**

ENCOURAGE SOMEONE—Download the message/chapter above for someone you know it would help.

·

CHAPTER NINE

Could your mental diet be killing your soul?

It is written: "Man does not live on bread alone,
but on every word that comes from the mouth of God." [1]
—*Jesus of Nazareth*

I was recently talking with a friend about a documentary he just watched with his children. Someone decided to test the quality of food in one of America's most famous fast-food restaurants. The thirty-day plan was to eat nothing but fast food morning, noon, and evening. Tests were done prior to the experiment and would be done after the experiment to evaluate levels of fat, triglycerides, weight gain, and overall health.

Unfortunately the experiment did not last thirty days. After twenty or so days of a steady diet of only fast food, the man's body began to shut down. The high-sugar, high-fat, fried, and processed food began to build up toxins to such a degree that he had to be hospitalized. Ironically the food tasted great; tragically it almost killed him.

Tastes Great but It Might Kill You

Sometimes what tastes great isn't very good for us. And what researchers tell us is that we acquire a taste for certain foods (like sugars and sweets) that can actually become addicting. It may look good, smell good, and taste good, but that doesn't mean it is good. All those foods promise pleasure, enjoyment, and fun (and an occasional burger never hurt anyone), but a steady diet of foods high in calories, high in fat, and low in nutrition will literally kill you. As someone has wisely said, "We are what we eat!"

What most Christians don't realize is that the same is true spiritually. If we fill our minds with the world's value system (like we discussed in chapter eight—the lust of the flesh, lust of the eyes, and the pride of life), we will die. We will experience death or separation in our relationship with God, ourselves, and others. Like fast food, it tastes good, looks good, and promises a wonderful time only to deliver death. In order for us to enjoy and get the very best from God, it requires a change in our diet. In the last two chapters we talked about the negative command in Romans 12:2—"Do not be conformed to this world." In this chapter we will look at the positive command—"*be transformed by the renewing of your mind.*"

God's solution for genuine transformation is not rules. It's not simply an emphasis on all the things we are not to do. God's solution is not trying hard to be more moral or to keep one's spiritual nose clean through self-effort. In fact, God's solution is not primarily about religious activities or programs. Although they have their place and benefits when properly understood, church attendance and church programs are unable in and of themselves to produce lasting life change.

No, supernatural transformation is rooted in our spiritual diet. The battleground (as we learned in the last chapter) for your soul is in your mind. Satan uses the world system to seduce your flesh primarily through the use of lies and deception about what will satisfy and fulfill the deepest longings of your heart. That gate to your heart is your mind. The most important decision you make every day is what you allow to go into your mind! If you think I'm exaggerating, take a closer look at the positive command in Romans 12: 2: "Do not be conformed any longer to the pattern of this world, but be transformed by the renewing of your mind." The verb *transformed* comes from the Greek word *metamorphosis*. The prefix *meta* means "with" and *morphosis* means "to change."

Metamorphosis: Results of a Spiritual Diet That Really Works

Metamorphosis is that process of transformation that happens from the inside out. The beautiful butterfly we all enjoy with its bright colors and distinctive markings was once a small green worm crawling up a branch. Then the transformation process begins shortly after it enters into a brand-new environment called a cocoon. The green worm is transformed over time from the inside out into a beautiful butterfly. This is what science calls "metamorphosis." This unusual word is also used in Mark 9, where it says, "Jesus was transfigured before them."

Jesus had taken His three closest followers up on a mountain, where they met Moses and Elijah and heard God's voice authenticating Jesus as the Son of God. In the midst of that experience, the text says, He was "metamorphosised" before them. This passage does not teach that a bright light from heaven was shining on Jesus; but a light far brighter than the sun was shining "out of Him" as He unveiled His glory and deity to Peter, John, and James. The primary point I want to make is that life change—genuine spiritual maturity—is not the result of external self-effort, but a supernatural process that flows from the inside out. To better understand how this process works in our lives we need to carefully examine the grammar of verse 2.

> Do not conform any longer to the pattern of this world, but be transformed by the renewing of your mind. Then you will be able to test and approve what God's will is—his good, pleasing and perfect will.
>
> —ROMANS 12:2 NIV

POSITIVE COMMAND: ". . . BUT BE TRANSFORMED BY THE RENEWING OF YOUR MIND."

"Be transformed"

- Passive voice
- Imperative
- Present tense

This verb—"transformed" (metamorphosis) is in the passive voice—indicating God is the one who does this in our lives. It is also an imperative—a command so we have a real responsibility in colaboring with God in this transformation process. And finally this verb is in the present tense—it is a continuing ongoing process. The following expanded translation will give you a sense of what the grammar indicates:

Expanded Translation: "But allow God to completely change your *inward thinking* and *outward behavior* by cooperating wholeheartedly moment by moment with the Spirit's renewing process."

What most of us do not realize is that we are being transformed in our thinking all the time—either by the world's value system or by the truth of God's Word. The world's values bombard us daily with thousands of messages on billboards, in movies, songs, video games, and television programs that all reinforce a worldview that tells me life is about "me." Life is about what I can get, what I can achieve, who I can impress, what I can possess, where I live, what I drive, how much education I have, how much money I make, who knows my name, and how successful I am . . . and the list goes on.

By contrast, God uses His Spirit, His Word, nature, great books, and the authentic community of fellow believers to remind us that life is about "Him." And life in Christ is all about what I can give, who I can love, how God can use me, how significant and accepted I am regardless of what I make, where I live, what I drive, or who knows my name.

Renewal: The Power Food for Spiritual Transformation

You and I are living in a constant tug-of-war for our hearts and minds. Our God-given needs for significance, security, and belonging are constantly being pulled to seek fulfillment via the world or via the way of the Word. The most succinct explanation of why most Christians live lives of duplicity and inconsistency is primarily found in their spiritual diet. If my diet consists of a steady dose of prime-time television, movies, magazines, self-help books, and romance novels, I will believe that the world is "about me" and I will seek to achieve, perform, and work to make my life "work" for me. I can genuinely be born again, go to church, verbally express my love for God (and mean it), and have sincere intentions and desires to be "a good Christian" and yet live a life that bears little resemblance to that of Jesus Christ. Why? Because the transformation of a genuine child of God has everything to do with how we are "renewing our minds." So, let's take a closer look at what that means.

> The most succinct explanation of why most Christians live lives of duplicity and inconsistency is primarily found in their spiritual diet.

- *Renewing my mind is a continual refocus of a Romans 12:1 perspective.* My intake of God's Word, my reflections on nature, my times of worship and prayer, and interactions with fellow believers all serve to remind me that He is Lord and CEO of the universe. Each day I awaken to the reality that I have indeed surrendered to Him at a point in time; but today I offer my life afresh, surrendered to Him in order to fulfill His purposes and accomplish His will—not my own.
- *Renewing my mind will always involve a battle.* This world system, its architect Satan, and my flesh all conspire together to de-

ceive me with regard to who I am, where I belong, and why I'm here. Renewing my mind will require that I do spiritual battle and work at "taking every thought captive in obedience to Christ" (2 Corinthians 10:4–5).

- *Renewing my mind is a supernatural work of the Spirit of God.* I have a responsibility to set my mind on the things that are above (Colossians 3:1–4), but the actual transformation of my thinking is a work of the Spirit God—"For it is God who works in you to will and to act according to His good purpose" (Philippians 2:13). We must be careful not to fall into the faulty thinking that simply filling our heads with Bible verses or isolating ourselves from the evils of the world will necessarily produce the life of Christ in us.

- *Renewing my mind is always with a focus on love and relationship. At the heart of all renewing of the mind is the desire to know and enjoy Jesus.* Spirituality is never fundamentally about our external behavior but about our internal relationship that flows out into our external behavior. The religious leaders of Jesus' day demonstrated a stunning ability to be intellectually saturated with the Word of God, but completely missed a relationship with God. I think the Apostle Paul captures the relationship between renewing our minds and knowing Jesus best when he writes,

But we all, with unveiled face, beholding as in a mirror the glory of the Lord, are being transformed into the same image from glory to glory, just as from the Lord, the Spirit.
—2 CORINTHIANS 3:18 NASB

You see, the whole point of reading and studying God's Word and sharing life in community with other believers is to "behold Jesus for who He is"; to know Him, to enjoy Him, to love Him, and to be loved by Him. It is in this process of actually seeing and encountering Jesus that we are transformed. One of Jesus' closest disciples would later write:

> *Beloved, now we are children of God, and it has not appeared as yet what we will be. We know that when He appears, we will be like Him, because we will see Him just as He is.*
>
> —1 JOHN 3:2 NASB

So often Christians are told that reading the Bible is important, but I'm convinced most don't know why. Bible reading for many has become little more than fulfilling a duty, relieving some guilt, and hoping like a magic bullet it will bring good luck. So how do we interact with God's Word in a way that is relationally focused? How do we balance limiting the world's messages and seductions, but not become isolated, out of touch, religious weirdos?

Well, let's get practical. What does your mental diet look like? What are you putting in your mind? What do you think is the ratio between the amount of time you spend in God's Word or listening to the truth and the amount of time you take in messages from the world via TV, movies, and your computer?

Please don't gloss over the last few questions. I am not down on you and neither is God. These questions are not designed to make you feel guilty, but to help you get an accurate assessment of your mental diet. You are what you eat! As I've counseled with numerous people over the years, I have yet to meet a man or woman who does not experience radical and amazing life change over time when they change their mental diet.

How I "Jump-Started" My Mental Diet

In chapter eight, I shared my struggle with lust. I was a prisoner and no amount of self-effort delivered me. No matter how many times I pleaded with God, asked for forgiveness, and made promises about my future behavior, I continually experienced defeat until I changed my mental diet. I did not understand the spiritual principles of transformation that I'm sharing with you today. I discovered them quite by accident.

My roommate at the time was preparing to go to a summer training program with a parachurch organization. One of the requirements to attend this summer training program was to memorize sixty verses from the Navigator's "Topical Memory System." They were written on small cards and covered thirty categories of the Christian life. There were two key verses for each category and he was required to memorize the verses as well as the scriptural address (book and verse). Don't ask me why, but one day when he left the room, I decided to pull out his verses, write them on 3x5 cards, and memorize all of them before he did. Although my motives had nothing to do with improving my spiritual life and everything to do with competing with my roommate and winning, God used them for good.

Thanks to one extremely boring class I had in college, I found myself memorizing one verse every day and reviewing the verses I had memorized while sitting in the back of the classroom pretending to be listening. One of the requirements of the training program was that you review all the verses daily for sixty days so that you would retain 100 percent of what you memorized. I will never forget what happened on day 21. With twenty-one verses from the Bible in my heart, I was walking across campus when I ran into one particularly attractive girl on whom I had a crush. She was also the source of a significant amount of my personal guilt, as she was a very godly young woman and also the object of much of my lusting. I can't remember exactly what we talked about, but I remember vividly walking back to my dorm room in total shock. I didn't lust for her. My eyes were focused on her as a person and not as an object. None of the normal thoughts or struggles came into my mind while speaking with her or immediately afterward. I experienced victory! I had just won a battle that I normally lost 99 percent of the time. What happened? That was awesome! *It's possible!* I thought to myself, I really do not have to be controlled by lust.

It wasn't long before I made the connection between my newfound victory and memorizing Scripture. I learned that victory could be experienced not only in the area of lust, but with pleasing people, workaholism, pride, jealousy, worry, and a host of other issues. As time went on I began to get very serious about renewing my mind both by memorizing Scripture and studying it for myself. I began to look at specific areas of need in my life and find promises in God's Word that I could claim, memorize, meditate on, and then watch transformation occur.

Transformation is not only possible, it is commanded. And God never commands us to do anything for the fulfillment of which He doesn't provide the power and the resources. Do I ever lust, ever worry, ever exhibit pride or jealousy? Of course, these things still raise their ugly heads in my life on occasion, but they are the exception now and not the rule. I'm no longer a prisoner of those things and they no longer characterize my general lifestyle. We will never be perfect in this life, but we can progressively and consistently be transformed as we grow in holiness and love.

IT'S YOUR MOVE—Become an ⊙12 Christian

So how does it work? Where do you begin? What do you read? What do you study? Should I memorize some verses before others? How do you keep this from becoming legalistic? How do you ever find time to renew your mind when your life is already overflowing with demands? Well, that's what we'll talk about in the next chapter.

THINK—What action is commanded in Romans 12:2 that results in transformation? How does this action differ from ways you have attempted to be more Christ-like?

REFLECT—How would you characterize your mental and spiritual diet? What correlation might there be between areas where you "struggle" and what is going into your mind?

UNDERSTAND—What is your biggest barrier in renewing your mind?

- Don't know where to begin?
- Don't have a plan?
- Don't have the discipline?

SURRENDER—Ask God to create an appetite in your heart for Him and His Word. Ask Him to show you where to read in the Bible.

TAKE ACTION—Set your alarm clock back twenty minutes each day for two weeks and meet with God to start your day.

MOTIVATION—Listen to "Peace and Power of a Prioritized Life," which shows you a simple but powerful way to read and hear God's voice. **LivingontheEdge.org/r12.**

ENCOURAGE SOMEONE—Ask someone to make the two-week commitment with you to meet with God first daily. Text each other at noon in order to hold each other accountable!

CHAPTER TEN

.

Are you tired of "trying hard" and feeling guilty?

If you hold to my teaching, you are really my disciples.
Then you will know the truth,
and the truth will set you free.[1]
—*Jesus of Nazareth*

In a deeply personal letter, the Apostle Paul writes to his young son in the faith Timothy, urging him to walk with God in the midst of the moral cesspool of his day. Timothy was a young pastor in a city known for its red-light districts. Temples abounded on every corner to get any kind of sex you wanted—male and female prostitutes were available day and night. Living in Ephesus was like having a XXX porn site as the screen saver on your computer.

And it was into this environment Paul would write, "It is God who saved us and chose us to live a holy life . . ." and ". . . those who claim they belong to the Lord must turn away from all wickedness." Moral compromise was simply not an option in the New Testament church. The Apostle Peter was just as emphatic in his letters: "As obedient children do not conform to the evil desires you had when you lived in ignorance. But just as he who called you is holy, so be holy in all your behavior; for it is written: be holy, because I am holy" (1 Peter 1:14–16). The early church that changed the world was marked by two distinct characteristics:

1. Radical, self-sacrificing love for one another
2. Lifestyles of holiness and moral purity winsomely lived out with no air of self-righteousness or legalism

The question is how did they do it? That's what we want to talk about in this chapter. After much personal failure and counseling Christians for twenty-five years, I am convinced that most of us have relied on willpower, self-effort, and religious activities in our attempts to live a holy life. And eventually when we figure out that those things don't work, we do one of two things: we start faking that we're holy and develop lives of duplicity and hypocrisy, or we simply agree with one another that "the bar of holiness" is too high. We convince ourselves and one another that God doesn't really expect us to live up to such impossible standards.

Holiness has become relative in our day, allowing us to lower the bar and pick and choose which commandments we will obey. The result over the last few decades has been disastrous. Unbelievers mock the immorality of TV preachers and coworkers. Vibrant, New Testament Christianity has been repackaged and marketed to the lowest common denominator with few demands and outrageous promises. The Christianity that defined "true religion as looking after orphans and widows in their distress and keeping oneself from being polluted by the world" (James 1:27) has been replaced by a cultural Christianity that turns Jesus into our personal self-help genie to achieve worldly success, self-actualization, and above all else "personal happiness." This perverted brand of our historic faith has left authentic followers longing for intimacy with God and unbelievers with very few "living epistles" to point them to the revolutionary message of "Christ in us the hope of glory."

I do not believe that the majority of Christ-followers have willfully turned their back on the living Lord. We are a product of what we hear and what we believe. For many, their spiritual instruction and experience did not deliver the truth or the tools for genuine transformation. They have a spiritual longing and desire to really change—but they don't know how. For others, the small steps of compromise have snowballed over the years and left them hurt and cynical. Still others have been so wounded and disillusioned by the hypocrisy and unchristian attitudes in their institutional church experience that they simply have "given up on church," but still desperately long for God and the life Jesus promised.

Spiritual Growth ≠ Trying Hard

So, how does genuine life change (spiritual transformation that produces lives of love and holiness) really happen? If most Christians aren't living "like Christians," then something is fundamentally flawed in our understanding of the spiritual life. I want to help you to think differently about spiritual growth. I want you to begin to grasp that spiritual growth is not performance-oriented but relational. I want you to learn the difference between trusting God and His promises and trying hard in your own energy to be a "good Christian." I want you to break free of the old wineskins of cultural Christianity and experience God's infinite grace and furious love deep within your soul. So think carefully with me as we explore how spiritual maturity really works.

Let me make a few simple observations about what spiritual growth *is* and what it is *not*:

1. Spiritual growth *does not* begin with focusing on behavior.
2. Spiritual growth *does not* even begin with focusing on our attitudes.
3. Spiritual growth *always begins* by focusing on our thinking.
4. Spiritual growth *is accomplished* by the Spirit of God, through the Word of God, in the context of authentic community, for the purpose of glorifying God.

5. Spiritual growth *demands* that we by faith appropriate the grace of God given to us through the conduits of His Spirit, His Word, and His People.

So you see, only God can change us; but He never does it alone. The focus is not on trying hard to change our behavior; we can't do it. Focusing on our behavior is a dead end. When we attempt to become Christ-like through simply changing our behavior, it results in one of two outcomes: For those with an exceptionally strong will, it leads to external conformity to a set of rules, legalism, and eventually self-righteousness. The Pharisees were a good example of this brand of spirituality. But for most people, focusing on behavior leads to frustration and failure. Repeated unsuccessful attempts to change one's behavior or keep the rules result in despair or hypocrisy. This represents much of the Christianity in the twenty-first century.

Spiritual Growth = Renewing Your Mind

The focus in genuine transformation isn't even on trying to change our attitudes—"I shouldn't think that way, I shouldn't feel that way, I'm too judgmental, I should be more loving, etc., etc." Focusing on the "oughts" and "shoulds" of our attitudes only brings condemnation. There is a time and a place to focus on attitude, but it's not where to start. The place we must begin is our thinking! "As a man thinks in his heart so is he," wrote Solomon, the wisest man in the world. Romans 12:2 does not teach us to no longer be conformed to this world but to be transformed by some religious activity, a set of rules, or sincere self-effort; it says "be transformed" by the renewing of your mind.

If trying hard, being disciplined, or doing religious activities could break the power of sin and really change your life, many of us would win awards. We try desperately to change our behavior that we know is ungodly. We beat ourselves up continually trying to "have a better attitude."

Let me share a story that will help you understand the power of re-newing your mind. Early in our marriage, Theresa and I had multiple conflicts about my getting home on time for dinner. It may not sound like a big deal, but I would be perpetually late about once a week. She would have the meal fixed, the kids around the table, I would be late, the food would get cold, she would get hot, and then we would argue when I got home. Almost every time I was late for dinner, my excuse was basketball. I would jump into a great pickup game on my way home, and if we won the game, I needed to stay on to play the next one or I would let my teammates down. In my mind, I justified this because I was going to seminary full-time, working full-time, trying to be a good dad to three small children, and this was a rare hour or two each week that I did something for me. Theresa could not understand how walking off the court after winning a game was simply not an option. I couldn't understand why missing dinner once every week or so was such a big deal to her. So we fought. And as ridiculous as it may sound to you, we fought a lot.

Behind the conflict was a mind-set. It was about me exerting my rights and my personal time for me. I thought she was unreasonable and simply needed to understand. "So what if I eat some cold food now and then—it was worth it to me." That's the way I thought about it and I couldn't understand why she continued to get so upset. I tried to change my behavior and failed repeatedly. I didn't want the conflict, but down deep my thinking hadn't changed. I came home early a few times and conformed externally, but my effort was always short-lived. I told myself that I shouldn't be so selfish, that even though I didn't understand, I should be a kind and loving husband. In other words, I beat myself up for not having a better attitude—but that didn't work either. Then one day something happened that (renewed my mind) changed my thinking so profoundly that coming home on time was rarely ever a problem again.

I was taking a course in seminary on counseling and was convicted by God that I should give my life and lay it down for my wife (Ephesians 5:22–33). The truth of God's Word pierced my heart and I began to pray for wisdom to know how to "love Theresa in a way that made sense to her." I even wrote that phrase on a 3x5 card and carried it around in my pocket. In addition, Theresa had been learning how to share her anger in a more appropriate way using what we call "I feel" messages. In the past, when I walked in the door late, I was greeted by someone visibly angry who began telling me what I "should do" and "should not do" and what I "ought to do." Those messages sounded a lot more like a mother talking to her son than a wife talking to her husband. I responded to them with anger and defensiveness, which only poured more gasoline onto the fire of our conflict.

With that background, imagine what it was like when I came home late for dinner only to find the candles lit on the table and my wife in a pleasant mood. I seriously wondered what had happened, what was wrong. I had even prepared myself for a good argument while driving home. But there were no "oughts" or "shoulds" to argue with—only a woman under control, acting pleasant, and serving me dinner that she'd reheated. After five or six minutes of watching me eat, she asked if she could share something with me. I said, "Sure, go ahead." I will never forget what came out of her mouth as she quietly and calmly gave me an "I feel" message. "Chip, I feel deeply hurt and like you do not love me when I spend the entire day cooking a special meal to express how much you mean to me, and then you show up an hour late and miss it." No yelling, no demanding, she simply shared how she felt. It was as if a knife had been plunged into my heart as I heard those words.

I never thought about her cooking a meal as a message of love toward me. I never thought that I was hurting her. I thought I was only inconveniencing her and that she was angry because I was playing basketball. In that moment, my mind was renewed. I began thinking completely differently about an issue that had been the source of untold conflict in our relationship. The issue went from "trying to change my behavior to get home on time because I'm supposed to," to choosing to leave something very fun in order to communicate to the most important person in my life that I appreciated her sacrifice and her love for me. Without exaggeration, I was rarely late for dinner after that conversation. In an instant, in a flash, the truth of God's Word, "Husbands, love your wives as Christ loved the church," combined with the authentic community of my wife speaking the truth in love was used by the Holy Spirit to renew my mind—or to think completely differently about the situation. It was about love . . . not basketball. It was about love . . . not dinner. It was about love . . . not who was right.

Can you see what happens in our lives when we begin to think differently, think with God's perspective, and think in a way that focuses on relationship not rules or external behavior?

Can you imagine the freedom that you will begin to experience when you break free from the performance-oriented Christian life where the focus is on duty, attendance, spiritual disciplines, tithing, and guilt management with regard to all the things "you are supposed to do"? It's not that these things in and of themselves are bad, but for millions of Christians they've become little more than attempts at behavior modification accomplished through self-will and the energy of the flesh. I will tell you, it was easy to be on time once my mind was renewed. Basketball held very little attraction when weighed against my wife feeling unloved by me. It's the same in our relationship with Christ.

How to Renew Your Mind

So what needs to happen to allow us to look at things from that relational, "God deeply loves me" perspective? When excessive shopping, excessive eating, overworking, or visiting a porn site are all simply "things you are not supposed to do" because God says so, mentally . . .

you set yourself up to "try to do the right thing" when in reality you think/believe down deep that the shopping, working, eating, or lusting will give you what you really need. Nine times out of ten you will lose that battle. Willpower is no match for the lust and unmet needs that scream for relief.

But when your mind is renewed and the message is that you are so loved, so acceptable, such a delight to Jesus that He wants you to stay away from harmful activities that break His heart and ruin your relationship, it's a totally different story. The paradigm shifts from "trying to be good" by controlling your behavior to "expressing your love" by trusting in His promises.

How do we renew your mind? Well, it's really pretty simple. You must stop the flow of toxins into your thinking (i.e., media and ungodly relationships) and you must fill your mind (for the purpose of renewal—not performance) with the truth of God's Word, the beauty of God's creation, and the encouragement of God's people.

You will need to take some radical steps to shut off the supply lines of the bombarding messages of the world's values. You cannot continue to fill your mind with messages that promote the lust of the flesh, the lust of the eyes, and the pride of life. If you do, you will forever see God's commands as restrictions and unreasonable demands seeking to keep you from the "fun in life" and the things that will really satisfy. Unfortunately, this is how many Christians view the commands of God. Instead of guardrails to protect them and ensure they get the very best in life; they see them as fences and walls keeping them from where "the real action is." Then, seduced by the "real action and fun" of immorality, pornography, workaholism, unwise spending, and emotional affairs, they reap a life of sexually transmitted diseases, divorce, fractured families, over-

> The paradigm shifts from "trying to be good" by controlling your behavior to "expressing your love" by trusting in His promises.

whelming debt, guilt, shame, and addictions that hold them prisoners for life. The fallout is overwhelming; most Christians' lives are not working very well and it breaks God's heart.

God Longs to Renew You

If you are reaping some of the pain of your past, do not be discouraged. God longs to help you—beginning today. I have seen Him rescue addicts, broken families, workaholics, and seemingly impossible situations and do miracles. He wants you to be one of them. It will take hard work and some specific steps of faith, but there is hope and there is help as you begin looking at life with a renewed mind. It won't happen overnight and it will take some discipline. But after you experiment with your first media fast for three or four days and begin to renew your mind in fresh ways with God's Word, you will experience something really amazing—your thinking will change and as a result your desires and attitudes will follow. You will begin to see some behavior you've struggled with actually lose its appeal. As you shut down the supply of images and temptations and renew your mind with the truth, the Spirit of God will take the Word of God and make you more and more like Christ.

Jesus said, "If you abide in My Word you will know the truth, and the truth will set you free." Jesus prayed to His Father on the last night of His life for His followers: "Make them pure and holy by teaching them Your words of truth" (John 8:32; 17:17). In like manner, David would declare in Psalm 119:9, 11—"How can a young man keep his way pure? By living according to Your Word. I have hidden Your Word in my heart that I might not sin against You."

There are many books and great resources that provide excellent tools to help you renew your mind, but five things have been especially helpful for me.

Here are five specific ways to renew your mind with God's Word. I've included some practical, related resources that you can receive free of charge on our Web site (LivingontheEdge.org) to help you in this critical process.

The key, of course, is to remember that these tools are not an end in themselves or a means to gain God's favor, but a conduit of God's grace—to draw near in relationship and to personally experience His good, pleasing, and perfect will for your life.

Practical Methods for "Renewing Your Mind"

1. HEAR GOD'S WORD

Consequently, faith comes by hearing the message, and the message is heard through the word of Christ.

—ROMANS 10:17 NIV

2. READ GOD'S WORD

Blessed is the one who reads the words of prophecy, and blessed are those who hear it and take heart what is written, because the time is near.

—REVELATION 1:3 NIV

3. STUDY GOD'S WORD

Do your best to present yourself to God as one approved, a workman who does not need to be ashamed and who correctly handles the word of truth.

—2 TIMOTHY 2:15 NIV

4. MEMORIZE GOD'S WORD

How can a young man keep his way pure? By living according to your word. I have hidden your word in my heart that I might not sin against you.

—PSALM 119:9, 11

5. MEDITATE ON GOD'S WORD

Do not let this Book of the Law depart from your mouth; meditate on it day and night, so that you may be careful to do everything that is written in it. Then you will be prosperous and successful.

—JOSHUA 1:8

If you desire to learn more about how to specifically put these conduits of grace into practice, I recommend that you listen to the audio series *Ancient Paths to Intimacy with God* or read *The Miracle of Life Change*, both available at LivingontheEdge.org.

Once we understand this purpose in renewing our minds, our entire approach to church, Bible reading, fellowship, prayer, and spiritual disciplines completely changes. I don't "have to do them," it's not doing them that makes me acceptable or more loved by God . . . but they are the driveway to God's presence. I choose to do them to see life through God's perspective and remain aware of His love for me. When I miss church or prayer or reading my Bible, it's like missing a date with my wife because of a traffic jam. I don't feel guilty, I feel like I missed out. I love her, I enjoy her; I want to be with her.

In the end, "renewing my mind" is God's divine prescription for me getting the very best He has to offer. His will for me and you is characterized by three specific commands:

- *Good:* winsome, attractive, beautiful, richly satisfying
- *Pleasing:* acceptable to God and pleasing to us
- *Perfect:* according to design, maximizing our fullest potential in fulfilling God's purpose for our lives

IT'S YOUR MOVE—Become an ⊙12 Christian

Do you long to experience His will in your life? Would you like to know specifically what His will looks like for you personally? Why He made you with the personality you have, the gifts you possess, and what His purpose for you is? Well, in the next section we'll explore "How to Come to Grips with the Real You."

THINK—What did God say to you through this chapter?

REFLECT—What new insight did you get about how transformation occurs?

UNDERSTAND—Can you think of an experience where your "thinking changed" in a way that led to a change in a relationship or behavior?

SURRENDER—Ask God to renew your thinking about His commands—moving from restrictions to guardrails.

TAKE ACTION—Choose one of the five means of renewing your mind and start it this week. Consider memorizing Romans 12 as a lifelong reminder of becoming an r12 Christian.

MOTIVATION—Listen to part two of the series "Ancient Paths to Intimacy with God" at **LivingontheEdge.org/r12.** The message is called "How God Speaks to Ordinary People."

ENCOURAGE SOMEONE—Call someone today who has helped you grow spiritually and tell them what you learned about "renewing your mind."

B.I.O.

(BEFORE GOD DAILY, IN COMMUNITY WEEKLY, ON MISSION 24/7)

B.I.O. is the pathway to becoming an R12 disciple.

BEFORE GOD DAILY

As we talked about in this section, we are in a battle *everyday*. We constantly battle . . .

- our flesh (our old nature)
- Satan, who the Bible says has come to "steal and kill and destroy" (John 10:10 NASB)
- the world system, which warps our thinking, blinds our minds, and seduces our souls

It is so easy for our hearts to be wooed away from God and toward the world system. That's why Paul told us to "be transformed by the renewing of our minds" (Romans 12:2 NASB). Coming before God and renewing your mind with His truth is the antidote to the toxin of the world system. Ask God to create an appetite for His Word and make it your daily practice to come before God and marinate your heart and mind in Scripture.

IN COMMUNITY WEEKLY

Because the gravitational pull of the world's values is so strong we need other believers who can help us stand against the constant barrage of seductive temptations. With your small group have a discussion in which you identify some values of the world system that are contrary to God's values. Then have a candid discussion about where the world system is squeezing you and your family. Submit yourself to accountability from your group and ask for their help as you seek to live a holy and pure life. One of the action steps in this section is to do a media fast. If you haven't done this yet, consider getting your whole group to do a three- or five-day media fast together. A little positive peer pressure can be helpful when taking on a challenge like this. It will also allow your group to discover together the positive results of such a fast.

ON MISSION 24/7

Jesus said that we are to be in the world, but "not of the world" (John 15:19). We are not called to isolate ourselves. Being salt and light to our world requires proximity. Jesus beautifully modeled what it looks like to be *in* the world but not *of* the world. Jesus regularly rubbed shoulders with those far from God. The Bible says he was a friend of sinners. But He was different. He courageously and graciously resisted the value system of the world.

As you think about being separate from the world, don't let it push you to isolation. As we talked about in the last section, you are an ambassador. And as an ambassador, you are living right in the middle of a foreign land. But your values and assignment come from your king.

How to Come to Grips with the Real You

SOBER IN SELF-ASSESSMENT
ROMANS 12:3-8

Theological knowledge is the medium
through which the spirit flows into the human heart,
yet there must be humble penitence in the heart
before truth can produce faith.[1]
—*A. W. Tozer*

CHAPTER ELEVEN

Who do you think you are?

For everyone who exalts himself will be humbled,
and he who humbles himself will be exalted.[2]
—Jesus of Nazareth

The year was 1972. Without realizing it, I had begun a journey to answer the most important question of my life: "Who am I?" I don't mean this as some philosophical, abstract exercise in metaphysics, but I am talking about that deep sense of looking into the depth of your soul and knowing with certainty who you really are. This question is not always an easy one to answer, as there are many factors and many people who try to tell us who we are. To complicate matters even more, our desperate longing for approval drives us to seek, to look, act, and be what we think others want rather than discovering who we really are. It's a question we all grapple with and one that will determine in large measure the quality of our relationships and the level of contentment that we will experience in this life.

The Factors that Shape Our Lives

Our family background, our environment, our personalities, the significant others and role models of our childhood, the values and beliefs systems we were taught, all play a critical role in the formation of our self-identity. For example, I grew up in a middle-class home in central Ohio. My parents were both schoolteachers and my father was a Marine who served in the South Pacific at Guam and Iwo Jima during World War II. He was an excellent athlete, received a baseball scholarship to college, won the amateur boxing championship of the state of Virginia, was drafted by the St. Louis Browns baseball team after college, and lived the first fifty years of his life as a functioning alcoholic unable to overcome the atrocities he'd seen and the guilt he felt about killing so many people during the war. He wanted the best for me, but having lost his own father to gangrene when he was thirteen, he had difficulty communicating his love effectively to his children.

My mother was an incredibly loving, devoted, intelligent woman with amazing people skills. She was the glue of our family and unwittingly covered for my father in ways that enabled him and perpetuated a dysfunctional system in our relationships. That's a brief summary of my family background when viewed from a family-of-origin and psychological vantage point thirty years after the fact by a son who majored in psychology (me).

I had great parents who loved me deeply. They were the product of their family backgrounds, had lived through the Depression and World War II, and had raised me in the tumultuous decades of the late fifties to the early seventies. They provided, sacrificed, and gave their children all that they knew how to give, and I am forever grateful to them. I did not grow up in a Christian family whose members had a personal relationship with Christ or attended a Bible-believing church; I grew up in a religious and moral family that instilled high values and high self-esteem, and showed strong support.

Between my family background and the DNA that God sovereignly deposited in me, I grew up to be a highly motivated, deeply insecure, hardworking overachiever. With the best of intentions, my father expressed his love by wanting me to get the best out of life. His method for achieving this was through a highly performance-based ethic and by rewarding by means of conditional approval. All A's and one B on the report card would be followed by a significant discussion about what had gone wrong in the class in which I received a B. Getting two out of four hits in a baseball game would be followed by a discussion about what happened the two times I grounded out. The accomplishment of any goal or the achieving of any academic degree was followed by a brief smile and a discussion of the next goal and the next, higher degree. At this point in my life, I certainly do not share this in order to find fault with my father or to present myself as a victim in any way; I do so to help you understand that until you come to grips with how you were raised and how you responded to how you were raised, you will never discover the real you.

> Until you come to grips with how you were raised and how you responded to how you were raised, you will never discover the real you.

My desire to please and my father's performance-based rewards (along with strong support and love for my efforts) produced a highly driven, type A, goal-oriented workaholic with better-than-average people skills. I got good grades and earned an athletic scholarship to college. I learned to get what felt like love by fulfilling the expectations of others.

As I got older, I learned that different groups expected different things . . . so I became a social chameleon. I learned that when you're with girls in high school, you need to act sweet because that's important if you want to charm them and capture their hearts. I learned that when you're around teachers, you need to act like the all-American boy, say "yes, sir" and "no, sir" to get on their good side, and project a clean-cut image that will make for good references and a little extra grace when it comes to your grades. I learned in the locker room that you need to act tough, cuss like a sailor, and recruit the biggest, strongest guy on the team to be your best friend. Given my size, I needed someone to reinforce my contrived confidence and "don't mess with me" attitude.

You may be laughing by now as you read these words. Many of you, I'm sure, can identify with my desperate attempts "to be someone else" in order to gain the approval of others. Sadly, however, those immature best efforts never produced the desired results. When you're constantly pretending to be someone else, or attempting to gain others' approval by acting what you think they want you to be, you project what I call a "personality hologram" designed for image management. It's projecting a different you to different people at different times in the hope of being perceived as the kind of person they will accept, reward, and embrace. We all do this to some degree regardless of our station in life, but when it characterizes a person's basic approach to life and relationships, it is lethal.

We all hate hypocrisy—even when we see it in ourselves. By the time I was a senior in high school, I had become quite proficient in the art of image management. I had learned to deftly portray a "different Chip" to the various people and groups in my world. This produced a fairly significant amount of perceived success and a plethora of superficial relationships. But inside, I was dying. I was lonely. I was tired of pretending, but I didn't know what else to do. When the question "who am I really?" came to my mind, I simply didn't know the answer or even how to discover it.

In this section (chapters eleven through fifteen), I want to help you ask and answer the question "How do you come to grips with the real you?"

As I think about us going on this journey together to discover the real you, I can't help but get excited. Just a few weeks ago I shared this same material with about ten twentysomething-year-olds at a Bible study in my living room. Their honesty and questions were both revealing and affirming. As I watched them get extraordinarily excited in coming to grips with who God made them, I was reminded of how important it is to be real—how revolutionary it is when we can stop pretending and fully embrace "who we really are"!

I Saw Myself in Living Color . . . and It Wasn't Pretty

The breakthrough in my life occurred right after I graduated from high school. Although I was not a Christian at the time, the football coach at our school paid my way to go to a summer camp sponsored by the Fellowship of Christian Athletes. Each morning at camp prior to breakfast, we did a few exercises and then we were given about fifteen minutes to read the Bible. Since I had never read the Bible before, I was pretty slow in getting with the program, but by the fourth day I opened the Bible and read words spoken by God that launched my journey toward discovering who I really am . . .

> For by the grace given to me I say to every one of you: do not think of yourself more highly than you ought, but rather think of yourself with a sober judgment, in accordance with the measure of faith God has given you.
>
> —ROMANS 12:3 NIV

It's difficult to explain to another person exactly what happened in that moment. I had never read the Bible before and I certainly did not know what to expect. But as I read the words do not think of yourself more highly than you ought, the Holy Spirit pierced my heart (though I didn't know that's what was happening at the time) with the awareness of my arrogance and my pretended confidence.

As the words of Scripture lingered in my mind, I had an experience I will never forget. It was as though God pushed the video "play" button in my mind and I vividly saw previous encounters between myself and various groups in which I acted differently with each one. I saw myself in living color, acting sweet and kind to a beautiful young girl in our school while my real motives were simultaneously revealed. I saw pictures of me walking up to the front of the class and interacting with a teacher in my all-American boy persona to get one of my grades changed, and yet another picture from days earlier of me in the locker room spewing words of condemnation and sarcasm to fellow athletes in order to hide my fears and insecurities. It was weird! It was convicting! But probably more than anything else, it was revealing; I had a sense of emptiness, loneliness, and sadness that I had never fully faced. I certainly did not know what it meant to "think of myself with a sober judgment," but what I did know was that I didn't like me, I didn't like pretending, and, if it was possible, I wanted to know the answer to three little words: *Who am I?*

That was the beginning of my journey; how about you? Who are you really? We all pretend to some degree: How do you do it? When you look in the mirror, do you like who you see? Do you realize that the most attractive person in all the world is the person God uniquely made you to be? Wouldn't it be great to find out who that person is?

Well, if the answer is "yes," fasten your seat belt: that's what we are going to cover in the next few chapters. But before we go there, let me ask you to take a few moments to do some thinking, to share some of your thoughts with a friend, and to dig a little deeper.

IT'S YOUR MOVE—Become an e12 Christian

God longs to speak personally to you. Take two minutes and slowly read through the TRUST ME questions and suggestions for spiritual growth. Now sit quietly for three minutes and ask God which of those questions or actions are pathways to grace that will strengthen and encourage you. Don't feel compelled to answer all the questions or do all that is suggested; listen to the Holy Spirit and follow His lead.

THINK—What went through your mind as you read this chapter?

REFLECT—What parts of my story could you identify with? What aspects of your story are difficult?

UNDERSTAND—When was the last time you thought seriously about the question "Who am I?" What part of answering this question makes you uncomfortable? Excited? Afraid?

SURRENDER—Ask God to help you see yourself the way He sees you.

TAKE ACTION—Write down the top three people and events that you think have most shaped how you view yourself today.

MOTIVATION—Watch the thirteen-minute video on r12 online "How to Come to Grips with the Real You" at **Living ontheEdge.org/r12.**

ENCOURAGE SOMEONE—Think of someone who has a low or untrue view of themselves and share two positive character qualities you see in their life. Tell them it's an assignment for a spiritual formation project you're working on so they don't feel awkward.

CHAPTER TWELVE

Have you answered life's biggest questions?

You are the ones who justify yourselves in the eyes of men,
but God knows your hearts.
What is highly valued among men is detestable in God's sight.[1]
—*Jesus of Nazareth*

Human beings (either consciously or unconsciously) are always seeking the answers to three fundamental questions in life.

1. Who am I? This question deals with our identity.
2. Where do I belong? This question deals with our security.
3. What am I supposed to do? This question deals with our significance.

When you think about it, how we answer these three questions forms the basis of how we live all of our lives.

Three Fundamental Questions

WHO AM I?

Take the first question for example: "Who am I?" This refers to how we generally think of ourselves and tend to introduce ourselves to others. The answers vary depending on the person. Who am I? I'm a doctor, I'm an athlete, or I'm a housewife. When I was small and ready to leave the house, my father often exhorted me to remember, "You're an In-gram," so make sure you act like one. All of these references to our-selves have to do with identity. As we grow older and life changes, we constantly reframe in our mind and in our communication who we are. But notice that nearly all of the words of identification we most commonly use in reference to ourselves really have to do with what we do, not with who we are.

WHERE DO I BELONG?

The second question we all ask is "Where do I belong?" This question deals with security. From the time we start to walk to the time we need a walker, we join clubs, are members of cliques, get tattoos, and buy designer clothes to communicate to others where we belong. On any given Saturday during football season, flags and decals on cars throughout the Atlanta area proudly proclaim the identity of the per-son they belong to. I'm a Georgia Bulldog with red flags waving, or I'm an Auburn Tiger with orange decals plastered over the back wind-shield, or I'm a Georgia Tech Yellow Jacket. Grown men wear football and basketball jerseys of their favorite players to declare their identifi-cation with a certain team, while grown women spend thousands of dollars on handbags to display a designer's symbol that bespeaks ele-gance and affluence.

We are all desperate to belong and we want others to know what family, what group, what country club, what gang, what political party, what socioeconomic class, what fraternity or sorority, what eth-nicity, or what church we are a part of in order to fulfill our need for security.

WHAT AM I SUPPOSED TO DO WITH MY LIFE?

The third question we ask focuses on the issue of significance: "What am I supposed to do with my life?" "Why am I here on this planet?" From the time that we are small children to well into midlife, we ask and we answer this question. Philosophers, theologians, and religions of all stripes develop different answers to this question—for it is indeed the fundamental question of life.

These three questions are the cornerstones of our entire existence. Unfortunately, in our day, the bondage to media and the noise of a fast-paced life often drown out our soul's cry to honestly answer these fundamental questions.

For many, much of life is spent refusing to face these questions, because to do so requires deep thinking and that leads to moral responsibility. The "God question" cannot be avoided when you ask, "Why am I here?" And even those of us who profess a love for God and a trust in Jesus Christ often skim over these questions. It is far easier to accept predigested religious answers and dive into energizing religious activities than it is to work through the sometimes painful and difficult process of "being still and knowing He is God." But quietness and stillness are required in order for God to tell you who you are, why you're here, and what you're supposed to do.

Why Is It So Difficult to Answer These Three Questions?

So why is it so hard to stop and face these questions? Why is it so hard to ask and answer three simple questions? Why is it that different people come up with so many different answers to these questions? Why do intelligent people find it so difficult to discover who they are, where they belong, and what they're supposed to do?

Before we answer these questions, I want to ask you to join me on a brief journey to another time and another place where God specifically reveals why answering these three questions will always be difficult and a source of personal and relational confusion.

The scene is the garden and there's just one problem—sin has entered the world. The following account is God's first encounter with our first parents after they had willfully disobeyed his command. Notice, as you read the text slowly and carefully, the shift that occurs in the open, vulnerable, and loving relationship between God and Adam, and between God and Eve. Second, observe the relational dynamic sin introduces between the first husband and wife.

> *They heard the sound of the LORD God walking in the garden in the cool of the day, and the man and his wife hid themselves from the presence of the LORD God among the trees of the garden.*
>
> *Then the LORD God called to the man, and said to him, "Where are you?"*
>
> *He said, "I heard the sound of You in the garden, and I was afraid because I was naked; so I hid myself."*
>
> *And He said, "Who told you that you were naked? Have you eaten from the tree of which I commanded you not to eat?"*
>
> *The man said, "The woman whom You gave to be with me, she gave me from the tree, and I ate."*
>
> *Then the LORD God said to the woman, "What is this you have done?" And the woman said, "The serpent deceived me, and I ate."*
>
> —GENESIS 3:3–13 NASB

Since this is a very familiar story, I would ask you to suspend your preconceived ideas about it being only a story explaining how sin entered the world. In this brief exchange between God and Adam, and then later between Adam with Eve, we find a new pattern in relationships that will forever alter how we relate to God and one another. Until you clearly understand what really occurred in our relationship with God and between one another as a result of sin, you will never be able to answer life's deepest questions effectively.

Let's take a look at this passage together. It's the cool of the day and Adam hears the Lord walking in the garden and presumably coming toward him to share a time of fellowship. The text seems to indicate that this was a common practice at that time of day and Adam responds quite differently than in days past. The God who made him, loves him, and enjoys him, comes to spend some time with him and yet he does something very different—he hides! God called to the man and said to him, "Where are you?" This was not an informational question; it was diagnostic.

God obviously knew where Adam was, but he wanted Adam to answer the question "Where am I?" Adam's reply is revealing: "I heard the sound of you in the garden, and I was afraid because I was naked, so I hid myself." Notice the three key words: *afraid, naked,* and *hid.* What caused Adam's fear? Adam had a new self-awareness. He was aware that he was naked. For the first time in Adam's experience with God, there are parts of him that feel exposed, parts that he feels uncomfortable about allowing anyone else to see—even God.

Adam (with his new awareness of good and evil) knows instinctively that something is wrong, that he does not measure up: his new knowledge is accomplished by a never-before-experienced emotion called shame and his response is to hide. Adam's new sense of shame created fear, fear of rejection, and inadequacy, which led to a new behavioral pattern of "covering up" or hiding who he really was.

For the first time in human history, man's response to God's desire for fellowship is shame leading to fear, and it results in hiding. But the relational damage is not done. God asks a second diagnostic question: "Who told you that you are naked, have you eaten from the tree of which I commanded you not to eat?" It's well worth noting that God does not greet Adam with condemnation, but with a series of questions to help him come to grips with the reality of his own behavior. Adam's next response must have sent chills up his wife's spine. Instead of owning up to his behavior, Adam shifts the blame onto his wife and indirectly onto God: "The woman whom you gave to be with me, she gave me from the tree, and I ate." Translation—it's not my fault. Psychologically we call this denial and blame-shifting behavior.

God patiently listens to Adam's excuses and like a good counselor asks the one who is accused (Eve) about the accuracy of the charge. "And the Lord God said to the woman, 'What is this that you have done?' And the woman said, 'The serpent deceived me and I ate.' " It didn't take Eve long to learn from her husband. When confronted with the truth about her behavior, she likewise refuses to take responsibility and blames it directly on a third party (the serpent) and indirectly on God, who created all living things.

On the surface, we have a familiar Bible story that tells us about what theologians call "the Fall" or how sin entered the world. But beneath this familiar story emerge the three biggest obstacles that you and I will ever face in attempting to answer those three big questions of life: Who am I? Where do I belong? And what am I supposed to do? The Fall is far more than a theological concept. The Fall marred our relationship with God, our relationship with others, and our relationship with ourselves. And if you do not understand the implications of how this plays out, you will chase your tail spiritually for the rest of your life.

Three Barriers to Discovering the Real You

There are three specific obstacles to answering life's biggest questions:

1. *Fear rooted in shame.* We live out of fear in our relationship with God. We live out of fear in our relationship with people. We are afraid to fail and we are afraid to open up and be vulnerable because we fear people will see our inadequacy— that we don't measure up. As a result, we are afraid to be

honest, we're afraid to try, we're afraid to make a mistake, we're afraid to let people into our lives, and we are afraid to even look honestly at who we are. Why? Because like Adam, there are parts of us that we know do not measure up. All these fears become significant barriers and make it difficult to answer the question "Who am I?" It's an identity issue.

2. *Hiding rooted in insecurity.* Why did Adam hide? "I was naked and so I hid." Our sense of inadequacy and insecurity causes us to hide our true selves—not only from God but from one another. It goes something like this: if you really knew the "real Chip Ingram," not what I project, not the sanctified, cleaned-up part, but if you really knew the "real me" with some of the thoughts that I have, and some of the things I've done, you would reject me! I know in my soul that there's a discrepancy between who I want to be, who God calls me to be, and who I really am. But that discrepancy is far greater than I'm willing to share. And my greatest fear (left to my own resources) is that you'll see who I really am. I fear that you will see how inadequate and insecure I am behind all the positive images that I project and masks that I wear.

It is called image management. The issue is not whether you do it; it's how much of it you and I do. We're always projecting a better self. We seek to communicate, "I'm a hard worker," "I'm a good mom," "I'm a sincere Christian," "I'm generous," "I do this and I do that," "I met with so-and-so yesterday to help them when no one else cared," "I graduated from such and such a school," and the list goes on. This doesn't make us bad, it makes us human. We are fallen human beings and our relational patterns (apart from receiving Christ's work of redemption) will be to hide from God, ourselves, and one another because we are all desperately insecure.

3. *Blame rooted in denial.* When people uncover our "fig leaves" or God begins to ask us hard questions about our behavior or attitudes, we not only hide but we blame. Our insecurity is revealed and our sin is uncovered, so we instantly rationalize our actions by shifting blame to someone or something else. "It's not my fault . . . it was the family system in which I was raised." "It's not my fault . . . I was abused as a child" . . . or "the government let me down" . . . or "our educational system failed me" . . . or "Hollywood put all those evil thoughts in my mind" . . . or "my mate was frigid—I had to find love somewhere" . . . or "the church was not meeting my needs . . ." In both large and small ways, sophisticated and blatant ways, we blame something or someone else for our problems, failures, and deficiencies.

These three barriers, caused by sin's entrance into the world, make relationships impossible without God's help. And even after we have come to know Christ personally and having the penalty of our sin removed and the power of sin broken, it is a difficult and arduous journey to stop hiding and face our insecurities and blame-shifting tendencies.

These truths may be intellectually easy to grasp, but for me personally, they were very difficult to admit. The lifelong pattern of seeking to prove my value through my performance was deeply ingrained in my personality despite my new life in Christ. In addition, admitting that I was insecure felt like I was admitting that there was something wrong with me and I was weak. Although by the very definition of "confessing our sin" we declare that weakness and failure are true of us; at the practical level, being weak and insecure is not exactly the paradigm of manhood that I was ready to embrace.

How I Found the Real Me

The breakthrough for me happened when I was twenty-eight years old. It was my first ministry assignment at a small church in Kaufman, Texas. It was here that God brought me to the point where I could admit and recognize that I was insecure. God used the unique circumstances and people of this church along with a book by a Christian psychologist to break through my years of conditioning and false beliefs about my identity.

Although the church was named Country Bible Church and was located in a small town of about four thousand outside of Dallas, its founders were anything but country. I didn't know it at the time, but within a few months I realized the thirty-five people who made up this upstart church were not your typical small-town residents.

One man owned an insurance company, another family owned one of the largest and most prestigious CPA firms in Dallas, while yet a third owned real estate and a couple motorcycle dealerships and a construction company. When I went to visit their homes as the new young pastor, I realized that these were wealthy and influential people who had chosen to move to a nice small town to raise their families, but were anything but small-town people. Whether it was the size of their homes, the vacations they went on, or the cars that they drove, I was completely intimidated and felt desperately insecure in my new role as their pastor.

I grew up in a middle-class family. I remember, as a small child, all three of us kids sleeping in the same room of the two-bedroom house we rented. Somewhere along the line I learned to feel inferior when I was around people who had money. My father lost his dad during the

Depression and his death resulted in the family having to sell the farm and everything they owned. As a result, I grew up with an overdeveloped sense of frugality and at least a mild prejudice with regard to people of wealth. It wasn't anything that they did, but because of my insecurities and background, I felt small and dumb around wealthy people.

I felt self-conscious and inadequate as I rubbed shoulders with them in this new environment. But as I got to know my parishioners, and started seeing some of the cracks and pain in their lives, marriages, and families, I began to privately realize that "these people are as messed-up as I am." These smart, wealthy, successful people had all the same kinds of problems and issues that I had. In fact, as I began to do some counseling with some of their children who were going through difficult times, and with couples whose marriages were faltering, I soon realized that wealthy people often have unique and more difficult problems than the rest of us.

> As I got to know my parishioners, I began to privately realize that "these people are as messed up as I am."

About the same time I came across a book called *The Strong and the Weak* by Christian psychologist Paul Tournier. The thesis of the book is simple. After years of counseling people of all backgrounds, Tournier came to the conclusion that everyone is desperately insecure. Some people demonstrate their insecurity with strong reactions while others demonstrate their insecurity with weak reactions. The rest of the book consists of stories of people with strong reactions and people with weak reactions who demonstrated their various levels of insecurity.

People who power up, come down on you hard, let you know quickly who they are and what they've done, tell you how many people report to them, how much they earn, and seek to impress you are desperately insecure. People with strong reactions like emotional outbursts, anger, tirades, and super-high control issues are exhibiting the defense mechanisms that some people use to keep others at a distance (or "to hide" in the words of Scripture) so that others will not see who they really are and reject them. This type of "strong" behavior keeps people at a distance so people can't see who they really are; they only perceive the projection of power and strength that hides the fear and insecurity behind the mask.

At the other end of the spectrum are people who hide their insecurities with weak reactions. Weak reactions include a wide variety of verbal and nonverbal cues that tell others, "I'm weak, I'm a victim, I'm super shy, I could never do anything of much importance, I'm afraid, feel sorry for me," etc. These weak reactions enlist support and concern in the early stages of a relationship, but after a while you try to help, and try to help, and pretty soon you simply distance yourself from them because you realize they don't really want help. Their weak reaction is another way of creating distance and hiding, so you never really get to know who they are. After recounting story after story, Tournier concluded that no matter how gifted, intelligent, or successful, all people had one thing in common: they were desperately insecure.

As I read this book, and observed the lives of the wonderful and wealthy people at my church (who had previously intimidated me to death), I came to the simple realization that I was insecure, they were insecure, and everyone I will ever meet is insecure as well. It was freeing beyond what I can explain. It gave me permission to take off my mask and be myself and help others do the same. It also helped me begin to recognize when I was posturing, pretending, or seeking to impress people because of my insecurity. It started me on a journey of reading and studying God's Word with fresh eyes to find my security in my relationship with Christ.

That was the beginning of a long journey that I'm still on, but I will tell you unequivocally that you can break the cycle of insecurity and learn to take off your mask and reveal the amazing and beautiful person whom God has made—namely you! The fears can be broken. The insecurities faced. You can learn to accept who God made you and then move forward in freedom, power, and joy.

I will never forget, fifteen years later, putting into practice the lessons I learned from that wonderful church about insecurities. I found myself in another very intimidating environment and I didn't know what to do. I was seated next to Chuck Swindoll at an event sponsored by the National Religious Broadcasters. It was a dinner by invitation only of national communicators and Christian leaders. It was the first one that I had ever been to and of all people to be seated next to—Chuck Swindoll! Living on the Edge had just begun as a radio ministry and I think we were on eight or nine stations at the time. So picture how intimidating it would be to sit next to one of your heroes in a room full of "spiritual giants" and you are the new kid on the block.

As I sat there with sweaty palms and my heart racing, I realized I was feeling very insecure and that I needed to apply what God had been teaching me over the last decade and a half. So I turned to Chuck and said, "Excuse me, Dr. Swindoll, my name is Chip Ingram and I'm real new to all of this. Can I tell you something before we get going here?" He said, "Sure." I said, "I'm really out of my league here, I don't know what I'm doing, and this is a very threatening environment. Do you think you could give me a few tips on how to handle myself and what to do as this broadcast ministry starts to grow?"

As I got this out of my mouth, about facing my insecurity rather than seeking to hide it, I felt my heart calm, the walls of fear evaporate, and I watched Chuck Swindoll scoot his chair over toward mine, put his arm around me, and say, "Chip, I know exactly how you feel, let me share a few things I think might be of some help that I've learned over the years. By the way, just call me Chuck." That first step, when I faced my insecurities in yet another new environment, began a relationship with Chuck Swindoll that has continued at that yearly dinner.

You see, we don't have to impress people. Who you are—who you really are is the most attractive person on the planet. And when we can learn to accept that because of "the Fall" everyone is desperately insecure, it frees us to take off our mask, be ourselves, and find our security in Christ.

IT'S YOUR MOVE—Become an ⊙12 Christian

You may be saying to yourself, *Great story, Chip. I'm really glad for you, but taking off my mask sounds pretty scary.* For others, this chapter may have "fired you up" as you realized you're not alone—you're just "normally insecure" like everyone else. Now you might be wondering, *How do I resist the temptations of pretending, blaming, and hiding? How do I discover the answers to those big questions: Who am I? Where do I belong? What am I supposed to do?* Those are the very issues we are going to talk about in the next chapter as we take a closer look at Romans 12:3–8. But before we do, take a moment to process what we've talked about in this chapter. Grab a cup of coffee or tea and let God speak to you as you reflect on the questions below.

THINK—What are the three barriers that keep us from discovering who we are? (Pp. 118–120)

REFLECT—How have you seen these barriers play out in your relationships?

UNDERSTAND—When and with whom do you have the greatest freedom to be yourself? In what situations do you find yourself projecting strong or weak reactions to keep people at a distance?

SURRENDER—Admit to God and yourself that you are desperately insecure and need to find your security in Christ—not in your appearance, performance, or possessions.

TAKE ACTION—Take off your mask with one trusted friend this week and discuss what you are learning in this chapter about how these three barriers play out in your life and relationships.

MOTIVATION—Download the audio message "How to Come to Grips with the Real You" at **LivingontheEdge.org/r12.**

ENCOURAGE SOMEONE—Choose to look beyond the irritating strong or weak reactions of someone you don't particularly enjoy being around. In the next few days, seek to understand why they are hiding, blaming, or pretending. Where possible, affirm the person hiding behind the mask by demonstrating the compassion of Christ.

CHAPTER THIRTEEN

Have you discovered the real you?

My sheep listen to my voice; I know them, and they follow me.
I give them eternal life, and they shall never perish;
no one can snatch them out of my hand.[1]
—*Jesus of Nazareth*

How do you resist the temptation of pretending, blaming, and hiding?
How can you move beyond the feelings of insecurity that paralyze your
life and ruin your relationships? How can you accurately answer those
three big questions that determine your destiny?

God's Answer—Romans 12:3–8 NIV

1. ***Who are you?***
   For by the grace given me I say to every one of you: Do not think
   of yourself more highly than you ought, but rather think of your-
   self with sober judgment, in accordance with the measure of faith
   God has given you. (verse 3)

THE COMMAND = THINK ACCURATELY ABOUT YOURSELF.

2. **Where do you belong?**
   Just as each of us has one body with many members, and these members do not all have the same function, so in Christ we who are many form one body, and each member belongs to all the others. (verses 4–5)

THE REASON = _____.

3. **What are you supposed to do?**
   We have different gifts, according to the grace given us. If a man's gift is prophesying, let him use it in proportion to his faith. If it is serving, let him serve; if it is teaching, let him teach; if it is encouraging, let him encourage; if it is contributing to the needs of others, let him give generously; if it is leadership, let him govern diligently; if it is showing mercy, let him do it cheerfully. (verses 6–8)

THE PRACTICE = _____.

Although we'll focus our energy in this chapter on discovering who are you? (v. 3), I want to make sure that you get a clear overview of this passage and see how it all fits together.

In this small section of Scripture, the Apostle Paul clearly lays out the answer to those three fundamental questions of life. He does it in the form of a command (v. 3), the reason for the command (vv. 4–5), and the specific practice of how to fulfill that command (vv. 6–8).

After eleven chapters that describe God's forgiveness, redemption, and indwelling by the Spirit, the text now reveals how our new relationship with Christ gives us a new identity, a new security, and a new and eternal significance. In short order, we learn there is a new way "to think," a new family "to belong" to, and a new purpose "to fulfill." In this chapter I want to help you understand how "to think accurately about yourself" as a child of God. You will never be able to take off your mask and connect deeply with others until you see and accept the "new *you* in Christ."

How Do You View Yourself?

I'm going to ask you to put on your thinking cap and really concentrate for the next few pages as we carefully examine what God is saying to you and me about our personal self-assessment in Romans 12:3. We need to move from general concepts to specific principles gleaned from God's Word to fully grasp how to overcome insecurity issues. So let's dig in together.

> For through the grace given to me I say to everyone among you not to think more highly of himself than he ought to think; but to think so as to have sound judgment, as God has allotted to each a measure of faith.
>
> —ROMANS 12:3 NASB

I want you to notice in verse 3 above that I have emphasized four specific portions. The main point of verse 3 is that God commands us to think accurately about ourselves. In fact, there is one root word that is repeated in various forms in this verse four times. Each time the word *think* and *sober judgment* is repeated, it is calling us to think about ourselves in a way that is consistent with reality. The phrase *sober judgment* emphasizes most graphically the idea of "not being drunk" or under some influence that would warp your perception of yourself. The apostle then goes on to give some specific warnings about how we tend to think wrongly or inaccurately about ourselves.

Notice it says, "Do not think too highly of yourself." This is an admonition against pride. Against the subtle feelings and self-perceptions that make us think we're more important than other people, smarter, of more value than those around us. Sometimes we do this in very overt ways, but in most cases, we do it in very subtle and sophisticated ways.

When I think too highly of myself, it always results in relational conflict and disunity. We've all been around people who carry themselves with an air of "I am God's gift to the world." It doesn't take us long to realize that we don't want to be around them. Yet in our honest moments, we all project these kinds of attitudes to others. Whether it's unexpressed anger toward someone who is not treating us with the importance and honor that we expect, or the impatience we feel when someone is not grasping what we want to communicate as quickly as we think they should; it's those subtle forms of superiority thinking that are prohibited in this text.

But the command is not simply a prohibitive, "not to think more highly of yourself than you ought to think"; he also gives a positive command, "to think of yourself with sober or accurate judgment." There's danger in seeing ourselves not only with an inflated view, but also with a deflated view. Someone has said, "Humility is not thinking too highly of yourself or too low of yourself; humility is not thinking of yourself at all."

We've all spent time with people whose words and body language scream, "I'm unworthy, I don't measure up, I'm a victim, you really wouldn't want to be around me if you knew what I was like, I can never do anything right, I'm a nobody going nowhere!"

Even after a brief amount of time with these people, we find ourselves listening to a multitude of messages designed unconsciously to elicit our support and compassion, but most often producing the opposite reaction. Don't get me wrong: there are real people with real problems who need our love as they go through difficult times. But what I'm talking about here is the kind of people who have an "I'm-a-nobody victim mentality." These people fit into the "extra grace required" category, and no matter how much encouragement or affirmation you give them, their warped perception of themselves keeps them a prisoner.

Just like the people who think too highly of themselves, this person's constant low view of himself has the same net result. *They are thinking about themselves.* And at the end of a day, whether it's high or low, an inaccurate view of ourselves results in pride. Pride, put most simply, is a preoccupation and a focus on ourselves.

Perhaps a word picture will help. I don't do much bowling anymore, but when I do, I've made an observation that's 100 percent consistent. If you throw the ball and it goes into the gutter on the left side, they call it a gutter ball and you get zero pins. If you throw a ball and it goes into the right gutter, it's called a gutter ball and you get zero pins. My point is, it doesn't matter which gutter (thinking too highly of yourself or thinking too lowly of yourself), they are both inaccurate views that are prohibited by God. Although this may sound strange to you, God actually commands you to think accurately about yourself. Well, how do you do that? The answer is in the last portion of verse 3.

Who You Really Are . . . in Christ

The phrase that immediately follows the command to have sober judgment, "according to the measure of the faith God has given you" is critical to our understanding of this passage. The word *faith* in this context does not refer to the subjective or personal faith that we have in Christ. The word *faith* here is used in an objective sense—i.e., the new life we possess in Christ—as "the faith" we all share as believers.

Newell, in his commentary on Romans, provides a great summary of the meaning of this phrase: " 'The measure of faith God gives you' refers to the standard by which one is to evaluate oneself, i.e., objective faith or a Biblical view of self." [2] So "the faith" in this context does not refer to our personal act of believing in Jesus, but refers to the objective reality of who you are in Christ and what is true of you because of your new relationship in Him.

This command to see ourselves "according to the measure of the faith" God has granted is a statement and summary of those truths articulated in the first eleven chapters of Romans. We are completely new creations when we put our trust in Jesus. Our old man dies, we receive the Holy Spirit, we have become an entirely new person (2 Corinthians 5:17) with a new standing and position before God. This call for an accurate view of self is to see yourself through the lens of Scripture.

I can't overemphasize this point because I think it is one of the most glaring omissions in the Body of Christ today. I meet Christians who love God and who long to follow Him with all their heart, but it is apparent that they have no real understanding of who they are in Christ. Their relationship is based solely on their experiences with God, but often not deeply rooted in the foundational truths of who they are and what they actually possess as a child of God. This lack of understanding destines sincere believers to defeat and frustration as they seek to live out the new life in their own power.

In like fashion, most new Christians are encouraged to get involved in Christian activities and begin the disciplines of the Christian life in order to grow spiritually. Church attendance, praying, reading God's Word, serving, and getting involved are the messages young Christians hear—and for good reason. It is critical that we talk to God from the heart, learn to hear His voice, have our mind renewed through His Word, and enjoy the fellowship of His people; but what is missing in all these valuable Christian "activities" is *specific teaching on what it means to be "in Christ."* We need to clearly understand how God sees us before we become inundated in activities for God. (If this hits home with you, I wrote a book called *The Miracle of Life Change* that could be very helpful to you.) Well, enough theology for now, let's get practical about how to see ourselves the way God sees us.

Seeing Yourself as God Sees You

The first ten years I was a Christian, I received great training in the "how-tos" of the Christian life. I learned to pray, get into God's Word, share my testimony, share the Gospel, and serve others by leading Bible studies and doing discipleship. But the thing that was missing in my life was an accurate view of myself—from God's perspective. I caught it in bits and pieces as I read the Bible and studied, but I had no clear understanding of how God viewed me or how to live out that truth. As a result, I spent the first decade of my Christian life trying to please God through my performance. I read, studied, served, and never felt like I measured up to God's standard. I would swing from feelings of condemnation and discouragement to ones of pride and self-righteousness depending on my performance. It wasn't until I discovered that I was already pleasing to God and didn't need to perform for God that I began to develop a sober self-assessment.

In my case, my insecurities led me to project and think too highly of myself, while the woman I married erred on the opposite side of the equation. In our marriage, Theresa and I found ourselves on a journey to learn how God actually sees us so that we could learn to communicate and actually make our marriage work. My inflated view of myself produced dysfunctions in our relationship just as her lack of self-worth and self-esteem did.

Early in our marriage, Theresa and I received some excellent marital counseling by a wise and godly pastor, who also worked part-time as a counselor. He gave us the tools and the understanding we needed to solve the day-to-day problems in our communication and relationship. But his real gift to us was helping us move beneath the surface and dig into the core issues of our identity in Christ. Dr. Richard Meyer helped Theresa and me learn "who we really were" in the eyes of God. He taught us how to have a sober self-assessment—not only of ourselves but of each other. As we learned together, our relationship began to blossom in ways that we never imagined.

Dr. Meyer created 3x5 cards for Theresa and me to review to help us see ourselves as God sees us in five critical areas of our life. I remember sitting on the couch early in the morning and reviewing these cards out loud with Theresa. We would review the cards daily, and little by little, our thinking began to change. Following are the five cards we reviewed for years, passed on to our children and countless others to help see themselves "according to the measure of faith given them by God."

Let me encourage you to read over the cards out loud, slowly and thoughtfully, every day for six weeks. Don't even try to memorize the cards or the verses; just slowly and audibly speak the words and ask God to help you begin to believe that what you're reading is actually true *about you*!

When we learn to get God's view of us—who we really are—everything begins to change. Because the fact is, we talk to ourselves multiple times a day—telling ourselves messages that influence how we think, how we relate, and what we do. If deep in your heart you feel unworthy, unloved, inadequate, or more important than anyone else, it will dictate what you do and how you relate to others. Most of these false beliefs are such deeply buried, lifelong patterns of thinking that it will take a rigorous plan and ongoing accountability to break them.

Change Is Possible for You!

Lest you think you can never change—you're wrong! Changing how you think about yourself may be hard work, but the rewards are well worth it. When my wife and I began reviewing these cards nearly thirty years ago, Theresa was a woman who was beautiful, but thought she was ugly; who was gracious and kind, but thought she didn't measure up; who was the most wonderful person I'd ever met, but felt inferior and had desperately low self-esteem. Then I watched her work and review these cards day after day. Little by little she began to believe what God said about her rather than the messages she'd absorbed from the people of her past and the traumatic experiences she had lived through. In the last thirty years, I've watched a flower bloom before my eyes. Today I live with a woman who is beautiful on the inside and the outside and has a clear sense of confidence and positive self-worth that comes from thinking accurately about herself.

APPEARANCE
My physical appearance (in my unchangeable aspects)
is beautiful in God's sight.
He is my designer and maker.

·

PSALM 139:13–17
For you created my inmost being; you knit me together
in my mother's womb. I praise you because I am fearfully and
wonderfully made; your works are wonderful;
I know that full well. My frame was not hidden from you
when I was made in the secret place.
When I was woven together in the depths of the earth,
your eyes saw my unformed body. All the days ordained
for me were written in your book before one of them came to be.
How precious to me are your thoughts, O God!
How vast is the sum of them!

BELONGINGNESS

I am wanted, appreciated and loved by God,
the most important person in my life.

•

ROMANS 8:31–32

What, then, shall we say in response to this? If God is for us,
who can be against us? He who did not spare his own Son,
but gave him [Jesus] up for us all—how will He [God the Father]
not also, along with him [Jesus], graciously give us all things?

(Also refer to Ephesians 1:18)

WORTHINESS

I am now a righteous person in God's sight
since I have trusted Christ.
I am covered by the robe of His purity and goodness.
Also, since I have a new nature, I am a good person in my general
practice of life as I continue to grow in Christ
(see 2 Corinthians 5:17).

•

ISAIAH 61:10

I will rejoice greatly in the Lord, my soul will exult in my God;
For He has clothed me with garments of salvation. He has
wrapped me with a robe of righteousness, as a bridegroom decks
himself with a garland, and as a bride adorns herself with her jewels.

SECURITY

I am secure in my relationship to Christ, in my daily
safety and well-being, and in my future outlook,
whether on earth or in Heaven.

·

ROMANS 8:38–39
*For I am convinced that neither death nor life, neither
angels nor demons, neither the present nor the future, nor
any powers, neither height nor depth, nor anything else in
all creation, will be able to separate us from the love of
God that is in Christ Jesus our Lord.*

COMPETENCE

I am a competent person, equipped by the Holy Spirit to carry out
God's will in my daily life in a way that pleases Him,
regardless of what stage of growth I may be in at the present.
My real importance in life is connected with the way
I am touching other people's lives
with the love of God and message of Christ.

·

PHILIPPIANS 2:13; 4:13
*For it is God who works in you to will and
to act according to his good purpose.
I can do everything through Him who gives me strength.*

·

EPHESIANS 2:10
*For we are God's workmanship, created in Christ Jesus to do
good works, which God prepared in advance for us to do.*

———

Let me encourage you ladies to take seriously what's written on these cards and find a partner who would be willing to review them along with you for the next six weeks. You will be absolutely amazed what occurs when you renew your mind with the truth and begin to think as you ought to think with a sober self-assessment.

And, men, I've made a special point to talk to the women because of my personal experience with Theresa, but I will tell you, these cards have done as much for me as they did for her. My warped view of myself didn't show up in the same way that Theresa's did, but it was in reviewing these truths that I came to the point where I could stop comparing and striving and finally learn to rest and enjoy who God made me, just the way I am.

IT'S YOUR MOVE—Become an ⊙12 Christian

So, what happens when you get an accurate view of yourself? Why is it so important that you see yourself accurately? How does that impact those around you? How does a sober self-assessment provide the answer to "Where do you belong?" That's the next chapter.

THINK—What is a sober self-assessment?

REFLECT—On a scale of one to ten, how accurately do you think your view of *yourself* is? Why?

UNDERSTAND—What is your understanding of your position in Christ? Do you think it is important to appropriate what you already possess (faith) versus trying hard to live up to God's standards?

SURRENDER—Ask God for the power to obey the command in Romans 12:3 to "think accurately about yourself."

TAKE ACTION—Make a copy of the cards in this chapter and review them daily for six weeks.

MOTIVATION—Ladies, if you need some hope, listen first-hand to my wife Theresa's story in her series "Precious in His Sight" at **LivingontheEdge.org/r12.** This teaching grew out of her own journey toward sober self-assessment.

ENCOURAGE SOMEONE—As you review these identity cards for the next six weeks, make an extra set and give them to a friend.

CHAPTER FOURTEEN

Where do you fit in God's family?

From everyone who has been given much,
much will be demanded;
and from the one who has been entrusted with much,
much more will be asked.[1]
—*Jesus of Nazareth*

Recently, I sat across the table from one of the most successful men I know. Every time his name comes up in Atlanta circles, the words that accompany that name and describe the man tend to be along the lines of *bright, capable, successful, smart, really knows how to make things happen*. Over the last couple of years, he's become a good friend and has helped me and the ministry immeasurably.

On this particular day, I saw another side of my friend. He was discouraged. It took me a while to pick it up because he's normally such an upbeat guy, but he was really down and actually said, "Chip, I'm really discouraged." It wasn't one of those "I had a bad day" kinds of discouragement or "I had a flat tire" or "I'm having a little struggle with one of my kids"; it was a foundational, core discouragement that weighed heavy on his heart.

I'll never forget what he shared. He said, "I feel adrift right now, I don't know where I belong." For a variety of reasons, my friend was experiencing a season in his life during which the places that he had been spiritually and the sense of belonging he had known were no longer a fit. The only problem was he didn't know what that "right fit" was.

My friend knew what he was good at, was praised for his successes, but still lacked one important thing . . . belongingness.

Belonging Is a God-Given Need

In his landmark book *Bowling Alone*, Robert Putnam makes the case that loneliness is America's new epidemic. People are searching for a place to belong. In the 1970s, it wasn't uncommon for someone to leave a job that paid well and go off into the woods in order to "find himself." The issue of the existential sixties and seventies was one of identity. Who am I and why am I here? The issue of the twenty-first century appears to be "where do I belong?"

Belonging is a God-given human need. We all need and want the security of belonging to a family, belonging to a group, belonging to a team, belonging with people who need us just like we need them in a healthy and productive way. The fragmentation of the family and the rapid growth in technology have made people more mobile and isolated than ever before. The aching need to belong is at an all-time high.

Nobody has capitalized on community like Starbucks. When they train their employees, they put great emphasis on how to provide a sense of belonging to their customers. One of my daughters-in-law worked for Starbucks in Chicago while my youngest son finished college in that city. In her training, she learned that Starbucks is the "third place." The first place is home, the second place is work, and the third place is where authentic community can occur—Starbucks. She learned, "We don't just sell coffee here, we create a place for authentic community to occur and where relationships can deepen." And, of course, when those things are happening, people sit and drink an awful lot of coffee, as is evidenced by the fifteen-thousand-plus Starbucks around the world.

So, what about you? Where do you belong? Where do you fit?

How do we answer this question of belonging in a way that moves beyond the electronic connections of texting and social networking? Where do we discover that place of belonging that transcends our personal peace and prosperity and touches the deepest core of our soul? What is it that we were made to do and where do we belong in such a way that parts of us come alive like never before?

In the last chapter, we talked about the issue of identity. We learned the key to discovering who we are begins with thinking of ourselves and seeing ourselves the way God does. But discovering your true identity without knowing where you belong is like getting all dressed up with nowhere to go. Romans 12:3 commands us to think accurately about ourselves, and the very next verse tells us why. I've reproduced the entire set of questions from the last chapter because it's critical that we understand that where we belong is dependent on thinking accurately about ourselves and later understanding what we're supposed to do.

God's Answer—Romans 12:3–8 NIV

1. *Who are you?*
   For by the grace given me I say to every one of you: Do not think of yourself more highly than you ought, but rather think of yourself with sober judgment, in accordance with the measure of faith God has given you. (verse 3)

THE COMMAND = THINK ACCURATELY ABOUT YOURSELF.

2. *Where do you belong?*
   Just as each of us has one body with many members, and these members do not all have the same function, so in Christ we who are many form one body, and each member belongs to all the others. (verses 4–5)

THE REASON = YOU HAVE A ROLE TO FULFILL!

3.   *What are you supposed to do?*
     We have different gifts, according to the grace given us. If a man's
     gift is prophesying, let him use it in proportion to his faith. If it is
     serving, let him serve; if it is teaching, let him teach; if it is encour-
     aging, let him encourage; if it is contributing to the needs of others,
     let him give generously; if it is leadership, let him govern diligently;
     if it is showing mercy, let him do it cheerfully. (verses 6–8)

THE PRACTICE = _____.

Once we learn to think accurately about ourselves, we are told the reason why: "For just as each of us has one body with many members, and
all the members do not have the same function, so we who are many
are one body in Christ and, individually, members of one another"
(Romans 12:4).

Did you notice the little word *just* at the beginning of verse 4? Omitted in this translation is a tiny word that precedes it; it's the Greek
preposition *gar,* which is translated "for." This small but important
preposition in Greek tells us why it's so critical to think accurately
about ourselves. The Apostle Paul uses a simile here and makes a com-
parison with the human body to make his point: "Just as the human
body has many members (eyes, nose, mouth, hands, legs, etc.) and
these members do not all have the same function, so in Christ, we who
are many form one body and we each belong to all of the others."

Every Person Has a Role to Fulfill

His point is very straightforward: As the human body has various individual parts with very specific functions that need one another, so

we, as members of the spiritual Body of Christ, have very specific abilities in order to function effectively. As the various parts of the human body (although extremely diverse in function) operate in interdependent unity to accomplish a purpose beyond the scope of any individual part, so the Body of Christ is to function as a team or family for the reality of the life of Christ to be manifest to its family and to the watching world.

The reason you need to think accurately about yourself and know who you really are is that *you have a role to fulfill* in this supernatural community of God called the "church." And don't get thrown by that word *church*, please. I'm not talking about buildings, brick and mortar, or organizations and services. I'm talking about the organic, supernatural functioning of individual Christians living in obedience and dependency to the head, Jesus Christ, in such a way that the spiritual body of individual believers is fulfilling the very same mission that Jesus fulfilled when He walked upon the earth.

And what was Jesus' purpose? Jesus came to "seek and save that which was lost" (Luke 19:10). Jesus came to explain the Father, full of grace and truth (John 1:18). His life revealed the holiness and unconditional love of God. Jesus' hands touched lepers and Jesus' eyes saw need and Jesus' feet moved toward people who were hurting. Jesus' tongue rebuked self-righteous religious people in one sentence and His tongue commanded the wind and the waves to be calmed in another. Jesus' physical body is now in heaven. He has a resurrection body complete with piercings and scars for all eternity to remind us of His love and the price of redemption.

But the work of Christ is now to be completed by His supernatural, spiritual body called the church, the Body of Christ. You belong to this supernatural, organic community of believers if you've placed your

You are needed! You have abilities and talents and background and experience and strengths that no one else in all the world has except you!

faith in Jesus Christ. You have a role to fulfill that no one else can fulfill like you. You are needed! You have abilities and talents and background and experience and strengths that no one else in all the world has except you! You also have needs that God wants to support and dysfunctions and pain that God wants to heal as you interact with other members of this supernatural community called the Body of Christ.

If you think too highly of yourself, you will not see your need for other people. If you think too lowly of yourself, you will not feel worthy to allow yourself to be loved by other people in the Body of Christ. But, if you think accurately about yourself, you will be a perfect candidate—not only to receive love but also to give it in the way God designed.

Every single person has certain strengths and certain weaknesses. We are born with them. They are natural abilities unique to our DNA. God has given you strengths in order to affirm your design, to give you confidence, and to allow you to make a contribution to the lives of others. For some of you, it's intellectual strength; for others, it's mechanical. For others, it's social or organizational strength. Your strengths help you define your role.

Watch Out for the Comparison Game

In like manner, we all have inherent weaknesses. Our weaknesses remind us that we need other people. Our weaknesses create opportunities to humble us and allow others to "wash our feet." Our weaknesses demand that we become dependent on other people by being vulnerable and open in our relationships with one another.

However, when we are unclear or have a distorted view of ourselves, we tend to compare our differences rather than appreciate them. We compete with one another rather than realizing we were made different (by divine design) so that we might complement and support one another. It is our insecurities that make us want to compare our gifts or talents with others. The result is always negative as we conclude that we are either superior or inferior. But check out the strong word used in Romans 12:4: "we *belong* to one another." Literally, "we belong to all the others."

This passage provides insight into that age-old issue of unity and diversity. We are one body—unity; and we have many members—diversity. The members don't all have the same function, but they share the same purpose. The purpose of the Body of Christ is stated succinctly in Ephesians 4:15–16:

> *But speaking the truth in love, we are to grow up in all aspects into Him who is the head, even Christ, from whom the whole body, being fitted and held together* by what every joint supplies, *according to the proper working of* each individual part, *causes* the growth of the body *for the* building up of itself in love.

God wants you to fully grasp who you are and where you belong. You may have felt rejected by your family, by a team, by a club, by people at work, or even by those who claim the name of Christ somewhere in your past. But God wants you to know that you belong to His family, that you are needed, that you have strengths by which to meet the needs of others, and you have needs that He has prepared others to meet for you.

Unfortunately, much of what you have just read has been relegated to "the ideal" about how the church "ought" to really operate. Unless you have been a part of a dynamic church or well-led small group, most people's church experience has not provided the sense of belonging that this passage describes.

But before we begin to blame the church—the institutional church—and take potshots at all that is wrong, I suggest that equal weight must fall upon our shoulders; individual Christians like you and me who have gladly bought into the consumer mind-set of the contemporary church.

Sadly, the mantra of the average believer in the contemporary church is, "Ask not what you can do for your church, but ask what your church can do for you." Our consumer attitude shows up as parents shop churches for the best-themed children's program ("I don't think we'll go to this church—we're looking for more of a Noah's Ark theme"). We've run from program to program and to the hottest new thing in the community to get our needs met and our kids helped with as little involvement as possible.

Becoming a Romans 12 Christian is not about slamming the pastor or taking potshots at sincere ministries' and churches' best efforts; it's seeing where we are today and putting into practice the raw and radical commands of Scripture in our own personal relational networks to become the kind of people Jesus called "salt and light."

The Power of Clarifying Your Strengths and Weaknesses

So as we move forward, I would like you to ask yourself, "What are my strengths and how am I using them in my relationships with other believers right now?" "What are my weaknesses and how am I inviting other believers into my life as I make myself vulnerable and ask for help right now?"

Where do you begin? Let me suggest that you look at the picture of the 3×5 card shown on the following page and do an exercise that I ask everyone to do when I go through this passage. On the left side of the card, write your top three strengths, as best you understand them. On the right side of the card, write your top three weaknesses.

Don't overanalyze this exercise. Simply jot down what you think are three things that you're good at and three things that seem to always cause you struggle. And remember, we're talking about strengths and weaknesses at this point—not spiritual gifts. We will get to that in the next chapter.

Identity issues begin with an accurate view of ourselves, *security issues* are addressed when we discover where we belong, and *significance issues* are resolved as we contemplate what we, individually, are designed by God to do. These latter will be developed in the next chapter.

YOUR STRENGTHS & WEAKNESSES

MY TOP 3 STRENGTHS	MY TOP 3 WEAKNESSES
1.	1.
2.	2.
3.	3.

Let me jot down my top three strengths and my top three weaknesses to give you an idea of how it might help you understand where you belong.

CHIP'S STRENGTHS & WEAKNESSES

MY TOP 3 STRENGTHS	MY TOP 3 WEAKNESSES
1. TEACHING	1. ADMINISTRATION
2. LEADING	2. MAINTAINING
3. COACHING	3. FIXING

Over the years, I've learned that I'm good at teaching, leading, and coaching. I'm strong with regard to people skills but weak when it comes to tasks and things. I'm terrible with details, with administration, and I hate maintaining things! My ability, or rather, inability to fix things is renowned in our home. By the time one of my sons was about ten years old, I would actually pay him to put together toys for his brothers and sister because for the life of me, I couldn't figure out how to do it.

In the early years of our marriage, my wife actually accused me of playing dumb to get out of work because (from her perspective) my inability bordered on the ridiculous. I'm just weak there; I don't comprehend how things fit together or how they work. But that weakness has also been a gift from God.

When I first pastored in California, we bought an older home in a small subdivision that needed a lot of work. Water would come through the roof and windows leaked when it rained, the dishwasher leaked every time we used it, and most of our appliances broke after the first couple years we lived there.

A man named Dick was a retired schoolteacher who could fix anything. Dick was also a very godly and wise man who was an elder in the church. Money was tight and hiring a repairman wasn't an option. So Dick and I spent a lot of hours together fixing things around my house. The joke was "Dick and I fixed this" or "Dick and I fixed that," which meant to everyone who knew me that I was holding the tools and driving back and forth to Home Depot as Dick did all the fixing.

Dick and I talked about a lot of issues during those times together. I think I was a help to Dick in some areas of his life, and he was certainly a help to me in learning to be the kind of dad and husband God wanted me to be and the kind of pastor I was learning to become. It was my need and my weakness that brought his strengths and his wisdom into my life. That's church! That's the Body of Christ functioning interdependently in a way where love is expressed and exchanged. If you don't know your strengths and you don't know your weaknesses, you will be very reticent to volunteer to help someone or unwilling to ask for it.

I wonder what would happen if every believer did the simple exercise of identifying their strengths and weaknesses? What if you saw your strengths as an opportunity to reach out to a friend (or perhaps someone who lives under the same roof) to extend your strengths as an act of love? Do you see the power of having a sober self-assessment?

If we don't know ourselves very well, we're far more likely to hide our weaknesses than we are to share them. Belonging isn't a result of wearing a colored jersey and identifying with the home team, nor is it finding a group of people who share some common activity like bowling, basketball, volleyball, knitting, or shopping. Real belonging transcends superficial social needs and happens when fellow believers function as the living body of Christ. It really begins with one strategic shift in our thinking. We must be the Church rather than go to church.

> We must be the Church rather than go to church.

IT'S YOUR MOVE—Become an ⊙12 Christian

We go to a building where the Word is proclaimed and the Lord is worshipped and we sit next to others of like mind and like heart. That is a good thing. But *that* good thing is not belonging. Church attendance is no substitute for interdependent, authentic community. If this strikes a chord in your heart, I've put some specific tools at the end of this chapter to help you begin discovering today "where you really belong."

THINK—What thought or concept was most important to you in this chapter? Why?

REFLECT—Do you know "where you belong"? What's good? What's missing?

UNDERSTAND—Was it easier to list your top three strengths or top three weaknesses? Why do you think that was true of you?

SURRENDER—Sit quietly before the Lord and thank Him for your strengths and your weaknesses. Open your hands (palms up) to offer to God afresh your strengths to serve His Body and your weaknesses to receive grace from others.

TAKE ACTION—Fill out the three-strengths-and-weaknesses card on page 149.

MOTIVATION—Ask two or three friends what they think your top three strengths are and compare them with what you wrote down.

ENCOURAGE SOMEONE—Jot a handwritten note to someone whose strengths have been God's love expression to some need in your life. Thank them for using their strengths to make Christ known to you.

CHAPTER FIFTEEN

Do you know God's purpose for your life?

His master replied, "Well done, good and faithful servant!
You have been faithful with a few things;
I will put you in charge of many things.
Come and share your master's happiness!"[1]
—*Jesus of Nazareth*

Some questions have more than one answer. In fact, some questions will be answered differently at different seasons in your life. I think that's the case with the big question *"What am I supposed to do?"* I remember asking that question when I was finishing high school . . . after college . . . after seminary . . . after pastoring for twenty years . . . after all my children were grown . . . and just eighteen months ago during a time of deep reflection and evaluation of my gifts and calling before the Lord.

How would you answer that question right now? What do you think you're supposed to do? In what season do you find yourself? What little voices play in the back of your mind that set expectations about what you do and why you do it? Although the answer to these questions will morph as we pass through various life stages and mature spiritually, at the core of these questions is *significance*. What makes life significant? What makes my life worth living? Why was I put on this earth, what mission am I supposed to accomplish?

I believe your purpose and your significance are two issues that are closely aligned. God has gifted and equipped you to fulfill a "good work" (a mission) that He has prepared for you before the foundations of the earth (Ephesians 2:10). The question of "what you're supposed to do" is not primarily a vocational one, but one of stewardship and purpose. The real issue, therefore, is to discover what God has entrusted to you in the way of spiritual gifts (stewardship) and the passions He has placed in your heart (purpose) to fulfill the "good work" He has uniquely prepared for you to do.

God has a mission for your life. It is a "good work" that you have been uniquely made and gifted to accomplish. Your greatest joy and most significant impact during your brief stay on earth will be directly related to your discovery and accomplishment of that "good work." In Romans 12:6–8, you will learn how God reveals and empowers you for what He has made you to do.

It's critical as we look at verses 6–8 that we view them in the context of the passage. The issue of significance and purpose can only be properly understood when we think accurately about ourselves and know where we belong.

God's Answer—Romans 12:3–8 NIV

1. **Who are you?**
   For by the grace given me I say to every one of you: Do not think of yourself more highly than you ought, but rather think of yourself with sober judgment, in accordance with the measure of faith God has given you. (verse 3)

THE COMMAND = THINK ACCURATELY ABOUT YOURSELF.

2. *Where do you belong?*
   Just as each of us has one body with many members, and these members do not all have the same function, so in Christ we who are many form one body, and each member belongs to all the others. (verses 4–5)

THE REASON = YOU HAVE A ROLE TO FULFILL!

3. *What are you supposed to do?*
   We have different gifts, according to the grace given us. If a man's gift is prophesying, let him use it in proportion to his faith. If it is serving, let him serve; if it is teaching, let him teach; if it is encouraging, let him encourage; if it is contributing to the needs of others, let him give generously; if it is leadership, let him govern diligently; if it is showing mercy, let him do it cheerfully. (verses 6–8)

THE PRACTICE = DISCOVER AND DEPLOY YOUR SPIRITUAL GIFTS.
After commanding us to have a sober self-assessment (because we all have a specific role to fulfill in the Body of Christ), the Apostle Paul now explains how to discover our role. In verse 6, he tells us that since we have gifts that differ according to the grace given to us, we should each exercise them accordingly. He then goes on to list seven specific gifts, followed by a clear emphasis on focusing on your primary spiritual gift.

We will discuss the meaning of various gifts and how to discover your spiritual gifts a bit later; but right now I want you to notice that the author's argument is about focus, not about discovery. He has told you *who you are* and *where you belong* in verses 3–5, and now he shifts his attention to give clear direction about *what you're supposed to do*.

In verses 6–8, we can summarize the Apostle Paul's directive very simply by stating it like this:

- *Question:* What are we supposed to do?
- *Answer:* Discover and deploy your spiritual gift to fulfill your role in the Body of Christ.

That's what you're supposed to do. Fulfilling this command will look different at different times in your life and at various levels of spiritual maturity, but the emphasis is clear. God has deposited into each of His children a supernatural ability to build up the lives of other people. When you came to Christ, you were taken out of the kingdom of darkness and placed in the Kingdom of Light. You were sealed with the Holy Spirit and baptized—or literally "placed into" this new supernatural community called "the Body of Christ." When Jesus rose from the dead, He demonstrated His victory over Satan, sin, and death by giving spiritual gifts to each one of his spiritual children (Ephesians 4:7–10).

Your spiritual gift will be one of the primary indicators of what God wants you to do with your life.

What Does God Want Me to Do with My Life?

Your spiritual gift will be one of the primary indicators of what God wants you to do with your life. It will not be the only indicator, but it will be a primary one. Your supernatural ability to build others up to fulfill God's purpose will be aligned with your passions, experience, natural abilities, personality, pain, adversity, and circumstances so that the Holy Spirit will show you in each season of life your unique contribution into the lives of others. As you spiritually mature you will learn to develop and deploy your primary spiritual gift in the way that results in unexplainable joy and exponentially increasing fruitfulness.

Few topics bring more discussion or controversy than talking about spiritual gifts. So often the conversation quickly jumps to which gifts are operating today and which gifts are not. In other circles, the conversation becomes a listing of thirty-five or forty specific gifts with long definitions followed by an inventory or a test in an effort to help church members discover their spiritual gifts. I've certainly used these inventories and tests in the past, but have discovered that the net effect is to develop people who are more educated about the nature of specific spiritual gifts but not necessarily better equipped to actually discover and use their own.

The focus of Romans 12:6–8 is an admonition to place your energy and time around your primary spiritual gift. The text is very direct and emphatic; because of *who you are* and *where you belong*; this is your responsibility. Think accurately, get relationally connected, and then discover and deploy your spiritual gift. That's the apostle's point. Spiritual gifts are not the same as natural strengths and weaknesses. There may be overlap in some areas, but strengths and weaknesses have to do with what you received at your physical birth. Spiritual gifts, by contrast, have to do with supernatural abilities given by God at your spiritual birth.

One of my passions in life has been studying how God grows His church. I developed a twelve-part teaching series called "How to Grow a High-Impact Church," which grew out of my study of Scripture and research of churches all around the world. A high-impact church grows in three distinct ways:

1. *Grows deep.* People are actually maturing and becoming Christlike
2. *Grows wide.* There is a steady stream of people putting their faith in Christ who didn't know Him before
3. *Makes impact.* The church is meeting some of the most significant social needs of the community, including poverty, education, and social injustice.

In my study of these high-impact churches, I found that there were twelve characteristics that nearly all had in common. Churches where people were coming to Christ on a regular basis, growing to maturity, and reaching out in powerful ways to the community almost always helped those in their church discover their spiritual gift and find a place to deploy it. As I was teaching this truth in Russia to a group of pastors about three or four years ago, they asked me, "How do you teach people to discover their spiritual gifts?" The need was so overwhelming that we added a special session at the conference. I did my best job "off the cuff" to go to the major "gift passages" and explain them to the pastors. But when I finished teaching, I was aware that what I had given them was woefully inadequate. One pastor came up to me and said, "When will you put together a DVD series that clearly explains how people can discover their primary spiritual gift?"

That request, by him and others, haunted me. I knew I needed to deliver something that was clear and practical that used only the Bible to teach people how to discover and develop their spiritual gifts. It's a long story, but God after nine months stirred my heart on an international flight to India to spend about twenty hours straight with every note, passage, and the three best books on spiritual gifts that I had in my study in order to crack the code. I later put four messages together called "Your Divine Design" that uses nothing but Scripture to help people discover their primary spiritual gift and the ministry gifts that normally cluster around that primary spiritual gift, and learn how to deploy those gifts in their present context.

The specific teaching that examines each of the gifts and helps you discover yours is beyond the scope of this chapter, but there are resources available at LivingontheEdge.org to help you start that discovery process. From what I have observed, most Christians do not know their primary spiritual gift and, as a result, have not discovered or clearly defined the "good work" that God has prepared for them to do.

Why Knowing Your Primary Spiritual Gift Is So Crucial

There are three reasons why I believe it's absolutely imperative for you to discover your primary spiritual gift.

1. *Your spiritual gift becomes the basis for making major priority decisions.* If you understand how God has supernaturally gifted you, it will begin to dictate where and how you spend your time. Countless sincere believers find themselves saying "yes" to every request made by others (often out of guilt) because they feel it's "the Christian thing to do." God does not want you to be involved in everything. He wants you to be willing to do whatever He calls you to do with a servant's heart, but He wants the majority of your time and energy focused on developing and deploying your spiritual gifts to fulfill your Ephesians 2:10 "mission."

Knowing your primary spiritual gift can turn the spiritual flashlight of your focus into a spiritual laser beam. In my early years as a pastor, I was unclear about what my primary spiritual gift was, although I knew it had something to do with communicating. So I spent all my energy doing everything for everyone. My insecurities led me to attempt to fulfill everyone's expectations. I did not have a sober self-assessment and it resulted in exhaustion, guilt, and ineffective ministry. As I discovered that my primary spiritual gift centered on the communication and proclamation of God's Word, I began to make very important priority decisions about what to do with my time. I began to block off two to three hours every morning and a complete day each week for sermon preparation. My priorities changed because I understood my primary spiritual gift; this gave me the ability and the power to say "no" to some other very good things and released me from my guilt and from expectations I felt from others.

2. *Your spiritual gift is an affirmation of God's love for you.* We give gifts to people because we love them. We give them gifts at Christmas and birthdays, and to people just because we feel like it. Gifts are

evidence that someone matters to us and we want them to have something of value. And gifts aren't earned—they're free. God has deposited within you a supernatural ability that He wants you to use. This gift will bring great joy to you and produce great fruit (a gift) in the lives of others. Each time you use your spiritual gift, God wants you to be reminded of how much He loves you.

3. *A proper understanding of your spiritual gift keeps the work of Christ central in your heart and mind.* Ephesians 4:7–10 describes the victory of Christ over sin, death, and the devil. The quote from Psalm 68 in that passage presents a picture of a victorious king or general sharing the spoils after returning home from battle. When you discover and deploy your spiritual gift, it is to be a reminder of what Christ has accomplished for . . . victory over sin, death, and the devil. Left to ourselves, we can make ministry about us, our group, our success, our growth. Spiritual gifts, properly understood, remind us that they are a gift from God that celebrate the finished work of Christ and that apart from Him, we can do nothing.

We began this chapter with some probing questions . . . "What am I supposed to do?" "Why am I here?" "What is my purpose?" The answer to these questions begins with a sober self-assessment—to think accurately about who you really are. They demand that we cease the exhausting and futile pursuit of self-fulfillment, self-actualization, and "success" as defined by this world's values. The journey will not be easy, but seeing ourselves as God does launches us into "belonging relationships" of interdependence, honesty, and vulnerability. As we learn to risk and love, letting others see the *real* us, we will need to discover and deploy our spiritual gift to fulfill that "good work" God prepared for us before the foundations of the world.

The result? You come to grips with the real you—you give and receive real love. You stop pretending and start living. Like the progressive opening of a flower reveals fuller and fuller beauty, you grasp with humility and awe that you are fearfully and wonderfully made. Regardless of what God calls you to do, your primary spiritual gift and the passions placed in your heart will be *the key* to finding yourself *in the place that you belong, doing the thing that you love,* and *making the impact that you were designed to make* for the glory of God.

IT'S YOUR MOVE—Become an ⊘12 Christian

As we close this section, there are three things you must never forget.

1. **God uniquely created you. You are eternally valuable.**
   For you created my inmost being; you knit me together in my mother's womb.

   I praise you because I am fearfully and wonderfully made; your works are wonderful, I know that full well.

   —PSALM 139:13–14

2. **God placed you in His family. You are unconditionally accepted.**
   And to know this love that surpasses knowledge—that you may be filled to the measure of all the fullness of God.

   Now to him who is able to do immeasurably more than all we ask or imagine, according to his power that is at work within us, to him be glory in the church and in Christ Jesus throughout all generations, for ever and ever! Amen.

   —EPHESIANS 3:19–21

3. **God gifted you to fulfill His purpose. You are uniquely significant.**
   For we are God's workmanship, created in Christ Jesus to do good works, which God prepared in advance for us to do.

   —EPHESIANS 2:10

THINK—What is the value of discovering and deploying your primary spiritual gift?

REFLECT—How have you thought about your spiritual gifts in the past?

- Highly important
- Somewhat important
- Mostly confused

UNDERSTAND—How clear are you on "what you are supposed to do" with your life? Do you feel motivated or confused by this question? What do you think your primary spiritual gift might be?

SURRENDER—Ask God to make clear what your Ephesians 2:10 "mission" is in this life. Tell Jesus you are willing to follow if He will show you what you are supposed to do (John 7:17).

TAKE ACTION—As a quick shortcut to "test the waters," ask yourself: "What do I love to do? What am I good at?" Then go try it for six weeks.

MOTIVATION—Do whatever it takes to discover your primary spiritual gift. Determine a time to listen to the full-length audio message "How to Discover Your Primary Spiritual Gift" from the series "Your Divine Design" at **LivingontheEdge.org/r12.**

Encourage SOMEONE—Send a gift card this week to someone whose spiritual gift God has used to impact your life. Thank them for using the gift God gave them.

B.I.O.

(BEFORE GOD DAILY, IN COMMUNITY WEEKLY, ON MISSION 24/7)

B.I.O. is the pathway to becoming an R12 disciple.

BEFORE GOD DAILY

Many Christians struggle with their identity. Our struggle with identity can be traced all the way back to the Garden of Eden. Because of Adam and Eve's sin, there are three major obstacles to us having a healthy identity.

1) Fear, rooted in shame. Like Adam, we don't feel as if we measure up. We are afraid of being exposed for who we really are.
2) Hiding, rooted in insecurity. All of us are insecure at some level. Our sense of inadequacy causes us to hide our true selves, not only from God but from one another. And that leads to image management.
3) Blame, rooted in denial. One of our defense mechanisms is to shift blame to someone or something else.

If we ever hope to break free from these obstacles we must do what Paul challenged and think of ourselves with "sober judgment"

(Romans 12:3 NIV). You must begin to think accurately about who you are in Christ. As you come before God daily and immerse yourself in His truth, you will begin to get God's perspective on your identity. You can learn to accept who God made you and then move forward in freedom, confidence, and joy.

As you come before God in the coming weeks, make a copy of the cards that we talked about in chapter 13. Read them every day and meditate on them for the next several weeks. Then, as you pray, ask God to help you see yourself the way He sees you.

IN COMMUNITY WEEKLY

Where do I belong? That is one of the most significant questions in life. No matter what our background or personality, we all long to belong. We all need and want the security that comes with *belonging*. And having an accurate view of ourselves is crucial to belonging. As I wrote earlier in this section, if you think too highly of yourself, you will not see your need for other people. If you think too lowly of yourself, you will not feel worthy to allow yourself to be loved by other people in the Body of Christ.

If you are a Christ follower, you belong to this community of believers called the church. In the passage we studied in this section, we learned that "each member belongs to all the others" (Romans 12:5 NIV). Biblically and theologically, the moment you become a Christian, you are connected to the church. But on a practical level, authentic community doesn't happen automatically. We have to take initiative, invest in relationships, and take the risk of being open and real.

ON MISSION 24/7

Being part of the body not only gives you a place to belong, but it also gives you a place where you can contribute and serve. You are needed! You have abilities and talents and background and experience and strengths that no one else in all the world has except you. Those

God-given gifts were entrusted to you so that you could participate in growing and building up the body of Christ.

Every Christ follower ought to ask, "What is my God-given assignment, and how can I steward the gifts and abilities that God has entrusted to me?" An R12 disciple is one who not only discovers their gifts, but also deploys them.

As a way to put this into action, why not try the exercise I mentioned earlier in this section? As a quick shortcut to test the waters, ask yourself: "What do I love to do? What am I good at?" Then go try it for six weeks. Just get started serving, and God will guide you to your sweet spot.

·

How to Experience Authentic Community

SERVING IN LOVE
ROMANS 12:9-13

Most of us go through life praying a little, planning a little,
jockeying for position,
hoping but never being quite certain of anything,
and always secretly afraid that we will miss the way.[1]
—*A. W. Tozer*

·

CHAPTER SIXTEEN

What is authentic community anyway?

When he saw the crowds, he had compassion on them,
because they were harassed and helpless,
like sheep without a shepherd.
—*Matthew 9:36*

The voice on the other end of the phone line was serious and solemn: "If you want to see your father before he dies, you need to get here as quickly as possible." Those were the words I heard as my father, at eighty-five, was close to death. I found myself on a plane within the next two hours and then in a rental car with two close friends pulling up to the Raleigh-Durham Hospital in North Carolina. I learned my father had been unconscious for some time, and because of pain medication, he had been delirious through much of the day. After comforting my stepmother, I entered his room and sat next to his bed, knowing this would be the last time I would get to see him on this side of heaven.

My dad was a good man, but deeply wounded. Although he had become a Christian in his mid-fifties, it had been very difficult for him to communicate his feelings and verbalize his love. I know he cared for me deeply and that he was proud of me, but I longed to hear that from his lips. Like every boy (no matter what age you happen to be) I yearned for the approval of my father and wanted so much to have that deep, meaningful conversation from the heart with him before he died. It was about 8 P.M. and my dad's wife, Evelyn (he had remarried after my mom had died), was heading home after a long day at the hospital. She gave me a kiss on the cheek and a hug as she walked out the door. Her eyes were sad and she knew Dad's last days were upon us.

Then something strange happened. I've heard about this in books and doctors tell me that it's not highly unusual, but my dad awakened and was completely lucid. For the next hour and a half, he was all there and we had "the talk" that we had both desired for so many years. Dad asked about my wife and about each of my kids and their kids. He asked me how I was feeling about some of the big transitions in my life and what I was concerned about and what made me most happy. We relived a lot of years and some of our best times together. From Little League ball games to some of the most difficult and painful events of our past—we shared hearts, man-to-man. In those last hours, my father clearly and powerfully communicated the things that were most important to him. He held nothing back. He knew he was going to die. He was ready to die, and he wanted to communicate what mattered most.

When you're going to die, you tell people the things that are absolutely most important to you. On the night Jesus knew that He was going to die, He did exactly the same thing that my father did. After washing His disciples' feet and modeling for them the message of His entire life, He gave them a new command:

A new command I give you: Love one another. As I have loved you, so you must love one another. By this all men will know that you are my disciples, if you love one another.

—JOHN 13:34–35 NIV

He commands them, not about strategy, or about doctrine, *but* about how they should treat one another. He commands them to *love* one another, in the same way that He loved them. He loved them unconditionally, sacrificially, openly, vulnerably, and when it wasn't convenient. He met them right where they were and loved them just as they were—believing in them when they didn't even believe in themselves. Jesus loved the disciples in such a radical, self-sacrificial manner that He was now calling them to emulate Him in their relationships with one another.

But why? Why was it so important that the disciples love one another the way that Jesus loved them? The answer: *that the world would know that God sent Jesus, His Son, to save and forgive them.* The greatest and most powerful apologetic in the entire world is not an argument out of a book, but the love Christians have for one another. When we radically and authentically love one another from the heart, the world stands back in awe and wonders, *What makes them care so deeply for one another?*

After Jesus gave them this new command, He shared the Passover with His disciples. The Passover that night would turn into the Lord's Supper, as He used the elements of the bread and the wine to communicate His love and sacrifice for them and for the entire world.

Shortly afterward, we have the opportunity to eavesdrop on another deep conversation between a father and son: the second person of the Trinity (Jesus), speaking to the Father on the last night of his life about what was most important to Him. Listen to what He says:

> *My prayer is not for them alone. I pray also for those who will believe in me through their message, that all of them may be one, Father, just as you are in me and I am in you.*
>
> *May they also be in us so that the world may believe that you have sent me. I have given them the glory that you gave me, that they may be one as we are one: I in them and you in me. May they be brought to complete unity to let the world know that you sent me and have loved them even as you have loved me.*
>
> *Father, I want those you have given me to be with me where I*

am, and to see my glory, the glory you have given me because you
loved me before the creation of the world.

—JOHN 17:20–24 NIV

Here, on the last night of Jesus' life on the earth, He gives *one new command* and He *prays one specific thing* with white-hot passion and intensity. He prays that the disciples will love one another radically and
that the Father will work in their relationships so that they might experience unity and authentic community with one another, in the
same way that the Father and the Son have authentic community with
each other.

And if you why wonder Jesus puts such focus on this request and
such passion into this prayer, it is because the credibility of Christianity would rise or fall on the basis of Jesus' followers' relationships with
one another. Jesus knew that the most powerful means of authenticating His true identity and God's greatest act of love for this fallen world
would be how His followers would love one another in everyday life.

When Authentic Community Became Real for Me

I was eighteen years old and a skeptic. As I shared earlier, I came to
know Christ at a Fellowship of Christian Athletes' camp in 1972. I was
a skinny young kid who had earned a basketball scholarship at a small
school and was at this camp primarily to hone my skills, not learn
about God. After three or four days of listening to the Bible and even
opening it on occasion, I was curious, but far from convinced. My religious experience had been anything but positive.

But after an afternoon workout, I had a powerful experience that
completely reshaped my view of Christianity. I found myself walking
behind the wide receiver for the Atlanta Falcons and the fullback for
the University of Illinois. I can still vividly remember the green gym

shorts the professional wide receiver was wearing and the sweaty cut-off football jersey the fullback was wearing as they walked off the practice field.

I watched this wide receiver, with bulging muscles, fame, and wealth, take a genuine interest in the fullback's life. I couldn't make out all that they were talking about except for the fact that the college athlete was sharing some deeply personal struggles. At one point, the pro put his arm around the massive shoulders of the sweaty fullback and began to communicate, in hushed tones, words of hope, love, and understanding. I could tell they were totally unaware of my presence as I followed several feet behind, but I could make out just enough of the conversation to watch, for the first time, a grown man love another grown man in a masculine way.

My view of Christianity prior to this camp was that it was primarily for women, people who need a crutch, and those who were weak. Somewhere along the line, I had bought into Karl Marx's view of religion—that it was an opiate for the masses, but certainly not something that I needed.

As I listened intently on the long walk across the practice field that day, an emotion began to stir in me for which I was unprepared. Watching a successful athlete love another man in a powerful and masculine way pierced through all my defenses and insecurities. I could feel tears welling up in my eyes and a set of emotions that were foreign to my experience. Before long, I was walking just a little bit closer, but staying far enough back not to disturb them. I wanted to hear what they were really talking about and to validate for myself the sincerity and vulnerability that I sensed was being exchanged.

By the time I'd reached the other end of the practice field, all I knew was that these two men had something that I wanted. I didn't know what it was at the time, and I didn't know how to get it; but what I did know was that I was an insecure, driven, over-the-top hypocrite who longed to be loved and accepted. I was tired of pretending and projecting that I was something that I knew I wasn't. I longed to find a place where I could just be *me* (whoever that was!) and be loved and accepted for just who I was. What actually happened as I walked across the field was that I heard the message of life because Jesus' prayer in John 17 was being answered before my eyes as I saw two Christ-followers love each other the way Jesus loved them.

Authentic community is powerful. *Authentic community* is something that we all long for. *Authentic community* goes way beyond simply being on a team or being a part of a club. Authentic community occurs when the real you shows up and meets real needs for the right reason in the right way. It's when the love of Christ is shared and exchanged with vulnerability, sacrifice, and devotion. It's a place where you can be just who you are and be loved in spite of your struggles, hang-ups, and idiosyncrasies.

As I shared earlier, later in that week at camp, I personally asked Jesus Christ to forgive me for my sin and to come into my life. I asked Him to make me the man that He wanted me to be. I believed the good news about Christ because I saw the good news lived out in a relationship between two ordinary people whose names I'll never know.

Why Is Authentic Community So Difficult to Find?

Unfortunately, most Christians don't experience biblical authentic community. Even with the rise of the small group movement, there's no guarantee that being in a small group will necessitate Christians loving Christians the way Jesus loved His disciples. I've been in some excellent small groups where the feeling of authentic community was palpable, but I've also been in some small groups where we discuss the Bible, enjoy some positive social relationships, and go about living not much differently after our time together than we lived before. Authentic community is extraordinarily powerful, but extraordinarily rare.

As we launch into this section of r12 Christianity together, I want you to know this is far from theoretical for me. While writing this book, I've gone through one of the most significant ministry transitions of my life. It's the first time in twenty-five years that I have not been the senior pastor of a local church. My role as a pastor provided me with the structure and the environment in which authentic community could occur on a regular basis—whether it was with staff members, close friends, or biweekly meetings with elders that included large chunks of times in the Scriptures, sharing, and praying. But when I didn't have this anymore, I realized how much I had taken for granted the in-depth, honest relationships we shared.

During this time, Theresa and I have experienced what I now believe many Christians experience as a "normal" way of life—periods of loneliness and disconnection as we searched for a place to belong. We visited various churches and found it to be one of the most frustrating and discouraging experiences of our lives. In the midst of it all, my daughter came up with an idea that proved to be God's answer to our prayer.

Annie was going to a great church in the Atlanta area that has a huge singles population. She'd met ten or twelve people in their mid-twenties who all longed to grow spiritually, but were at various levels of maturity and didn't know exactly how to move forward. Well, before long, my wife is cooking dinner every Monday night for "twelve of Annie's closest friends" and I'm opening the Scriptures and doing life with the next generation. All I can tell you is what started out as Bible study turned into an extended family. Joy and love grew out of our time together beyond anything I ever expected.

After two or three weeks of us getting to know one another, the sharing got deeper and more honest. Soon group members were meeting one another's needs, sharing from the heart, and crying out in prayer together. The other night, as Theresa was finishing up the dishes and we were cleaning up the house after everyone left, I had this overwhelming sense of peace. What a privilege it is to be a part of God's family and really do life from the heart with a group of people.

Later, as we turned off the lights and went to bed, I put my hands behind my head and began to consider what was so wonderful about the evening. What was it that was so good about being with these young adults over the last several weeks? Just before Theresa drifted off to sleep, I said, "You know, honey, tonight was a blast, wasn't it? Tonight reminded me of why God led us into ministry in the first place. Do you remember when we first started out thirty years ago and we had college students over at our house for Bible study? Do you remember how I would meet with the guys to disciple them and you would meet with the girls? That's what it felt like tonight. It wasn't just preparing messages or building buildings or creating systems or hiring staff or structuring organizations so people could be in a position to grow; it was just hands-on loving ordinary people and being loved by them, just as we are." We put our heads on the pillow that night with a renewed sense (after thirty years of ministry) of "this is what it's really all about."

I do not know where you are in your relationship with Christ or in your relationship with His church. But what I do know is that it breaks God's heart that only a small percentage of Christ-followers genuinely experience the kind of life-changing community I am talking about. Authentic community is what it looks like when Christians really love one another. God's plan and gift to His Body is not that we simply meet together weekly, listen to someone talk, sing some songs, work hard to be morally pure, or even perform in good deeds to help others. These things are certainly meant to be the overflow of our relationship with Christ, but I fear that far too many Christians do them yet live lonely, isolated lives, longing to be loved and accepted just for who they are.

IT'S YOUR MOVE—Become an ⊙12 Christian

God longs for you to experience authentic community and we're going to learn how that can happen for ordinary, everyday people just like you and me in the chapters ahead.

THINK—What did Jesus command and pray for His disciples?

REFLECT—Why do you think Jesus made such a point of focusing on our relationships with one another?

UNDERSTAND—What gets in the way of experiencing authentic community in *your* life?

- Too busy—no margin
- Religious activities
- Disconnected from other like-minded believers

SURRENDER—Are you in meaningful, growing, Christ-centered relationship with a handful of people? If not, will you ask God to show you what you need to do in order to move in that direction . . . or deepen what He has already provided for you?

TAKE ACTION—Declare war on isolation and superficial relationships in your life! Write out John 13:34–35 on a 3×5 card and commit to living it out as God leads you this week.

MOTIVATION—Consider watching the fourteen-minute video message "How to Experience Authentic Community" at r12 online (**LivingontheEdge.org/r12**).

ENCOURAGE SOMEONE—Make the first move this week. Initiate coffee, dinner, or dessert with someone(s) and talk about your common need/desire for authentic community.

•

CHAPTER SEVENTEEN

Why is God so serious about your authenticity?

A new command I give you: Love one another.
As I have loved you, so you must love one another.
By this all men will know that you are my disciples,
if you love one another.[1]
—*Jesus of Nazareth*

Not too long ago, a young couple from our small group of twenty-something-year-olds came over to meet with Theresa and me. They're working through and sorting out God's will for their relationship, so we spent about an hour and a half talking, evaluating, and sharing from God's Word and our past experience.

It's not a part of my job or "official ministry." I just like them. I want to be around them. I want to help them. I see such potential in their lives and it has been an untold joy to see them grow in their relationship with the Lord and each other over the last few months. My point: we're not doing religion and we're not simply involved in a church to be "involved"; we actually love one another and we're doing life together. And make no mistake: it's not about just us giving to them. They give back to us far more than they could know. What we're experiencing is authentic community. And authentic community doesn't happen by going to church or reading your Bible.

Authentic community, as we learned in the last chapter, is rare and powerful. Authentic community is not for the spiritual elite; it is God's will for every believer. But for you to experience authentic community, you must understand what it takes for authentic community to occur. In Romans 12:9–13, God explains exactly what is required for authentic community to happen. The outline is simple, as you can see below:

Authentic Community Occurs When . . .

- the real you (v. 9) . . .
- meets real needs (v. 10) . . .
- for the right reason (v. 11) . . .
- in the right way (vv. 12–13).

THE *REAL* YOU—(V. 9)

- *Authenticity*—"Let love be sincere."
- *Purity*—"Hate what is evil. Cling to what is good."

MEETS *REAL* NEEDS—(V. 10)

- *Devotion*—"Be devoted to one another in brotherly love."
- *Humility*—"Giving preference to one another in honor."

FOR THE *RIGHT* REASON—(V. 11)

- *Motive*—"Not lagging behind in diligence, fervent in spirit, serving the Lord."
- *Method*—"Genuine service to God is characterized by":
  - Diligence—excellence
  - Enthusiasm—passion

IN THE *RIGHT* WAY—(V. 12-13)

- *Upward Focus*—"Rejoicing in hope, persevering in tribulation, devoted to prayer."
- *Outward Focus*—"Contributing to the needs of the saints, practicing (pursuing) hospitality."

In this chapter, I want to talk about what it means for the *real you* to show up in your relationships with fellow believers. The prerequisites for genuine connection and love to occur in your relationships are authenticity and purity. Authenticity, you might say, "Where do you get that?" Well, I get the idea of authenticity from the phrase *let love be sincere.* In fact the word *sincere* literally means "without hypocrisy." The idea of purity comes from the second phrase, where it states, "Hate what is evil. Cling to what is good." As the flow of Romans 12 moves from getting a grasp on "who we really are" in God's eyes (verses 3–8) to our relationships with one another (verses 9–13), the words are strong and direct. The clustered participles in verses 9–13 take on the form of pithy, specific commands that hold the key to "how to" love one another the way Jesus loved his disciples.

As a pastor for many years, I'm well aware that people can get so busy doing ministry and going to quality programs in the church that they never have a handful of people that they do life with, who really know them and love them deeply. There are a lot of lonely, religious people who know Christ personally, but aren't experiencing authentic community.

How to Become the Real You

So, let's talk about why that is and how to change it. The *real you* refers to who we really are, not what we want people to think of us. That's authenticity. The real you has to show up—not a projection of what you want others to think. Love must be without hypocrisy. That word for "sincere" or "hypocrisy" is a Greek word that means literally "without a mask." In ancient Greek theater, all the actors were males. Each actor played multiple parts in a play or production. An actor might play the part of a woman, a child, and two or three men in the same play during ancient times. This was done through the use of masks; the actor could dress up as many different characters by wearing a certain mask to portray the face of a man, woman, or a child. Actors of this day had to learn to throw their voices or make themselves sound like different people of various genders and ages.

This word *mask* that was used in the Greek theater is the same word that the Holy Spirit directed the Apostle Paul to use in addressing the Roman church. The Greek culture was prevalent at the time and Roman Christians were certainly familiar with the theater of their day. And so Paul says (my loose translation): "For authentic community and genuine love to occur between two followers of Christ, we need to *take off our masks.* We need to stop projecting what we think others will like, and start being open and honest, and appropriately vulnerable." If there is a singular disease that ruins authentic community, it's that of hypocrisy. When our relationships are characterized by posturing, seeking to impress, acting as though we have it all together, or downright untruthfulness, we eliminate the possibility of authentic community.

I can never be loved unless people know who I really am—the real me, not who I'm pretending to be to gain people's approval. And the same is true for you. We're often afraid to go here because it is risky. The possibility of rejection is real, but that's the price tag for authentic community. It's risking rejection by being honest and authentic in relationships that allows me to experience genuine acceptance when the people in the group embrace and care for me despite my frailties, struggles, and emotional baggage. It is the Christ in us that others need to see, both in our strengths and in our weaknesses.

God Takes "Being Real" Very Seriously

Being real is an absolute necessity for authentic community to occur. In fact, God placed such a high value on authenticity in the early church that He chose to judge the very first sin (hypocrisy) recorded in the New Testament church with a severity that is hard to grasp by our twenty-first-century minds.

This story is told in Acts 5:1–11. Let me give you a brief overview so you get a feel for what was happening in that day in the early church. The church was growing by leaps and bounds. Thousands of people were coming to Christ and the needs of the church were mushrooming, as 80 percent of the early church was made up of slaves and people of low socioeconomic status. At the end of Acts 4, we're told about a wealthy man who owns a piece of property on the island of Cyprus and who gives it to the apostles in order to help meet the needs of this growing population of early Christians. His name is Barnabas, and he's been given the nickname "The Son of Encouragement." We learn later in the book that he's a very godly and generous man who surrendered his life to Christ. He's living a life separate from the world and wants to be used by God to love other people who are in need.

In this setting, Acts 5 opens with a story of a couple named Ananias and Sapphira. Apparently, word got out that the gift was given by Barnabas and his reputation in the early Christian community was very positive. Ananias and Sapphira, observing this phenomenon, came up with a secret plan whereby they could gain the esteem and the approval of the early church community, but avoid the cost of actually giving the full price of the property that they were about to sell. So they privately devised a plan to sell a piece of property and pretend that they gave all the money from the sale as an act of love and sacrifice to the community of believers.

There was just one problem—they held back a significant sum of the money in an attempt to "have their cake and eat it, too." What I mean by that is that they wanted to appear as godly and as generous as Barnabas, yet keep much of the profits from the sale of the property for themselves. In other words, they put on "a mask." They wanted to appear loving and generous without actually being loving and generous.

At this point the story really kicks into high drama. Ananias walks in and tells Peter the wonderful news of the gift that he wants to give to the church. Peter, given special revelation by the Lord, understands exactly what Ananias has done and asks him, "Ananias, why have you conspired to lie to the Holy Spirit? Before you sold the property, was it not yours? And after you sold the property, was not all the money yours to do with whatever you saw fit?" In other words, Peter is saying, "You didn't have to give the piece of property in the first place. Second, if you sold the piece of property, you didn't necessarily have to give it all to the church." The problem here is the issue of hypocrisy.

The sin of Ananias and Sapphira was an attempt to feign or fake love and spirituality for the approval of people. The judgment that fell on Ananias at the moment was shocking to the early church and is certainly shocking to me today. At that moment of hypocrisy, Ananias fell dead at Peter's feet and the young men came to carry him away.

A few hours later, when his wife, Sapphira, arrives, Peter seeks to find out if she was a part of the plot or simply an innocent bystander. So he asks her a question about the price of the property. After Peter ascertains that Sapphira was indeed a part of the deceptive plan, his words to her are similar to that spoken to her husband, " 'Why is it that you have agreed together to put the Spirit of the Lord to the test? Behold, the feet of those who have buried your husband are at the door and they shall carry you out as well.' And *she fell immediately at his feet* and breathed her last and the young men came in and found her dead, they carried her out, buried her beside her husband, and great fear came upon the whole church and upon all who heard of these things." That's Act 5:9–11 for you.

At the very heart of authentic community and loving one another is honesty. What God emphatically declared when He judged this first sin recorded in the New Testament church is that He has zero tolerance for hypocrisy. Talk about a sobering group experience! I can only imagine the impact this event had for the next several months (if not the next several years!). It was as though God were saying, "There will be no room for religious games in this new supernatural community called My church! Love, real love, will be the hallmark of this tiny band of believers whom I have chosen to change the course of history." You see, once people start pretending, the possibility of genuine love and deep relationships is impossible. God knew if there wasn't authenticity in relationship with people, then the relationships would be phony and Jesus' command in John 13 and His prayer in John 17 would never be a reality.

Can you imagine what would happen if God chose to judge, even for a day, His church in this way? Most churches would be morgues; there would be dead bodies everywhere. It was this sin, more than any other, that discredited the message of the Gospel and Christianity to me as a young man growing up. Now don't get me wrong, I know none of us is perfect. We are all hypocrites to some degree. We all project things and say things to make a bit more positive impression than is really true. Because we live in a fallen world, this will happen to some degree in all of us now and then; to do it unconsciously is one thing, but to willfully pretend and project is quite another.

I can tell you one thing, I have a long way to go but I long to be real and honest and appropriately vulnerable in my relationships with brothers and sisters in Christ. I am learning to own my stuff rather than cover it up. I ask Him to help me not to pretend to be more than I am or to give the appearance that I'm better or more godly than I know is true. I have learned that authentic community is impossible unless the *real me* shows up. And when I receive encouragement and support, it means very little unless it is a response to the real me and not to "the Chip" that I want people to see.

It Takes More Than Just Being Authentic . . . Purity Is a Must!

Authenticity is only part of the equation. The passage goes on to say, "Hate what is evil. Cling to what is good." It has been said that the one security against sin is being shocked by it. Carlisle wrote, "What we need to see is the infinite beauty of holiness and the infinite damned ability of sin." The roots of hypocrisy go beyond our psychological needs and desires to make a good impression. Much of the "mask wearing" among us in the Body of Christ is done to cover our willful, known disobedience to God from fellow believers. When I have hidden sin in my life, the *real me* can't show up because I'm hiding something, I have to pretend.

So many of us unknowingly ask the wrong questions when it comes to the issue of sin. The questions so many are asking are, "How close can I get to sin without crossing the line? What rating does a movie have to have so I can watch it without committing a sin? How much can I drink before it's a sin? How much money can I have before it's considered greed? How far can we go in this relationship before it's called sexual immorality? How much can we bend the truth or spin the story before it's a lie?" We all do this to some degree and it results in Christians who continue to cross lines and cross boundaries that violate their consciences. Once these patterns develop, little private sins begin to take on a life of their own in the secret compartments of our hearts. No one knows about them and it takes an enormous amount of energy to keep them hidden. The problem is that sin does not only impact us privately, but every unresolved issue before God will affect others because we are a spiritual, living organism; we "belong to one another" (Romans 12:5).

So here's how it gets played out in real life. As you meet with a group of fellow believers or with a close friend in Christ and begin to pray and talk about deep issues of the heart, you don't share what's really going on because there are areas in your life and your heart that must remain hidden. And so you begin to wear a mask. You begin to pretend. And the grace of God and the power of authentic community are not available to you, nor do you give this power to others. Relationships become more and more superficial, filled with Christian clichés and religious jargon. Your soul shrinks and the guilt rises. After a while you find you don't want to be around committed believers, hear God's Word, or participate in activities that force you to confront your hypocrisy. Loneliness and isolation become your silent partners, while God longs for you to come home, come clean, and be restored.

The phrase *hate what is evil* is very strong. The word *hate,* or, as it is sometimes translated in the Bible, *abhor,* is not a mild one. In fact, the best way to describe this is with a word picture. If you've ever gone out of town for two or three weeks and left milk, fruit, or something perishable in the refrigerator and then come back after the food has spoiled, you'll begin to catch the force of this word. Do you remember opening the refrigerator, only to be overwhelmed with that putrid smell that made you want to throw up—that's this word!

The issue is not how close to sin can you get; it's how close to purity and righteousness can you be? Again, Romans 12: 9–13 does not speak of sinless perfection, but it does speak of walking in honesty and integrity. *God's love flows through clean vessels*.

So, where are you at? How are you doing? Is there a private sin in your life that needs to come into the light? Are you tired of hiding? Tired of pretending, feeling guilty and alone?

Do you realize that your sin and mine doesn't merely affect us, but it affects everyone in our relational network? Few things are more devastating than to have fellowship with someone you "thought you knew" only to discover that there was "another life" that they were living that brings everything that you shared together into question. I remember as a seminary student volunteering at a church in the college ministry.

I would teach there on the weekends and Theresa and I would have the college students over to our house for Bible study and prayer during the week. Once a month I met with the pastor in charge of this ministry to pray, discuss strategy, and be discipled. Our last meeting was the most memorable for me. The pastor was especially encouraging that afternoon. He gave me honest feedback on my teaching, commended me for my pastor's heart, and, as we parted, even prayed for me in the fast-food restaurant where our meeting took place.

Can you imagine how I felt when I stopped by the church a few hours later to learn that right after our meeting ended, he left town with another man in the church's wife. Their affair led them to destroy two families. His young wife and newborn baby were victims of a good man who in a weak moment allowed sin to shatter their lives. I was devastated! The church was in shock! Private sin is an illusion.

IT'S YOUR MOVE—Become an ⦾12 Christian

Don't let the enemy fool you into thinking you're not hurting anyone but yourself. We need *you*—an authentic, clean, forgiven *you*—just as you need us!

THINK—What is necessary for the "real you" to show in your relationships?

REFLECT—Why do you think God judges the hypocrisy of Ananias and his wife so harshly? How or where are you most prone to wear a mask?

UNDERSTAND—What is the relationship between hypocrisy and purity? Is there any "secret sin" or temptation God might be speaking to you about?

SURRENDER—Pray Psalm 139:23–24:

> Search me, O God, and know my heart;
>> test me and know my anxious thoughts.
>
> See if there is any offensive way in me,
>> and lead me in the way everlasting.

Commit to respond to whatever the Holy Spirit reveals to you.

TAKE ACTION—We all struggle with sin and hypocrisy. Both are like bacteria; once brought into the light, their power to infect and inflict disease is removed. Bring any "secret sins" or temptations into the light of God's presence (1 John 1:9) and tell a trusted friend or pastor. "Confess your sins to one another that you might be healed" (James 5:16).

MOTIVATION—Consider downloading "Overcoming the Dragon of Lust—for Men" if you struggle with this issue (**LivingontheEdge.org/r12**).

ENCOURAGE YOUR PASTOR—E-mail, text, or drop a note to your pastor. It's no fun sharing "convicting messages" that protect the flock from hypocrisy and impurity. Thank him for his faithfulness and courage; let him know we all need the truthful messages along with the grace of God.

·

CHAPTER EIGHTEEN

Are you building relationships that will last a lifetime?

My command is this:
Love each other as I have loved you.
Greater love has no one than this,
that he lay down his life for his friends.[1]
—*Jesus of Nazareth*

The rewards and impact of authentic community are amazing, but it doesn't come cheaply. It takes more than the *real you* showing up, if you really want to experience the kind of love that Jesus talked about in your relationships. It requires the *real you* showing up and *meeting real needs* in the lives of others, not just the ones that are convenient, easy, or emotionally inexpensive. And yet, when by God's grace, we move out of our comfort zone and love others in ways that require time, energy, and sacrifice, there's a payoff that no amount of money can equal.

More Than Sipping Coffee and Sharing Bible Verses

I remember one of the first times Theresa and I had the chance to really experience what it means to meet a *real need*. Early on in our marriage, we were growing Christians, giving the first portion of our income to the Lord's work, involved in a small group, discipling others, and looking for opportunities to help those in need. We had just moved to Dallas, where I could attend seminary to prepare for vocational ministry. We moved into a government-subsidized apartment complex that was filled with seminary students, dental students, drug addicts, and all sorts of people who had one thing in common—economic need! It wasn't long before we befriended our upstairs neighbors. Pat had a small boy about the same age as Eric and Jason (my two oldest boys) and they spent hours playing together. Pat (a fellow believer) and Theresa became good friends and we were thrilled when Pat's second child was born, about a year after we met them. I never got to know her husband very well, as he was on the road a lot, but I do remember vividly coming home and being greeted by a very distraught Theresa. As it happened, Pat and her husband were having problems and Pat's husband had left her that morning. She had no money, no job, a newborn, and no way to pay her rent.

Theresa consoled Pat, prayed with her, and helped out with the kids. As it came time to pay our rent, Theresa and I had one of those conversations that you think "just might be God's will," but you're almost afraid that it is. As we talked late one night, we both sensed that God was moving us to pay Pat's rent so she wouldn't be evicted. This would buy her an additional month to make arrangements for her and her family's housing. The only problem was that if we paid Pat's rent, we couldn't pay ours. The timing of the two rent payments was about ten days apart and it certainly seemed like the height of insanity to pay her rent, knowing that we would be left with only ten dollars in our checking account. But in this case, despite our inner protests, the Spirit of God made it clear to Theresa and me that we should take a step of faith and *meet a real need* for our sister in Christ. It was not noble and we were not being super spiritual; the Lord had made it absolutely clear— it was merely a matter of obedience.

By faith, we paid the rent and I expected the Lord, in some wonderful way, to allow me to make extra money in the next ten days to pay for our rent. Unfortunately, our rent came due and we had no money. We had a grace period of three days, and on the final day, when I had come close to losing all hope and being more than a little upset with God, an envelope came in the mail. A check for a thousand dollars was in the envelope from a friend of a friend whom I had not seen in ten years. It only said that he was prompted while praying to find out where we lived, what we were doing, and to send this to us.

This was the first of many lessons God would teach us about faith and how He literally wants us "to lay down our lives for one another" (1 John 3:16). I previously thought things like this only happened in books and to "select spiritual giants in the faith." What we learned was that God is eager to act powerfully on our behalf when our motive is to meet the *real needs* of fellow Christ-followers.

Authentic community is more than sipping coffee and sharing Bible verses in a living room. It's more than being nice to one another in the hallways of the church and it's even more than dropping off food when someone has a baby or is coming home from the hospital. Authentic community demands that the real you meets real needs. Pat was overwhelmed by the grace that she experienced and profusely thanked us in tears as she held her brand-new baby in her arms. We were in awe of God's provision for us, after

> Authentic community demands that the real you meets real needs.

He had pushed us out of our comfort zone to believe that the God who created heaven and earth could take care of our needs if we were willing to trust Him in an effort to love someone else. As we learned in the last chapter, authentic community occurs when the *real you* meets *real needs* for the *right reason* in the *right way*. In this chapter, we want to learn how to specifically experience authentic community by meeting the *real needs* of others.

Authentic Community Occurs When . . .

- the real you (v. 9) . . .
- meets real needs (v. 10) . . .
- for the right reason (v. 11) . . .
- in the right way (vv. 12–13).

THE *REAL* YOU—(V. 9)

- *Authenticity*—"Let love be sincere."
- *Purity*—"Hate what is evil. Cling to what is good."

MEETS *REAL* NEEDS—(V. 10)

- *Devotion*—"Be devoted to one another in brotherly love."
- *Humility*—"Giving preference to one another in honor."

FOR THE *RIGHT* REASON—(V. 11)

- *Motive*—"Not lagging behind in diligence, fervent in spirit, serving the Lord."
- *Method*—"Genuine service to God is characterized by":
  - Diligence—excellence
  - Enthusiasm—passion

IN THE *RIGHT* WAY—(VV. 12-13)

- *Upward Focus*—"Rejoicing in hope, persevering in tribulation, devoted to prayer."
- *Outward Focus*—"Contributing to the needs of the saints, practicing (pursuing) hospitality."

Those two commands are simple but powerful. They focus on the two prerequisites for meeting the real needs of others, devotion and humility: "Be devoted to one another in brotherly love." What does it really mean to be devoted to one another in the Body of Christ? The word *devoted* here is the Greek word *philadelphia*. Its root meaning has to do with special and intimate affection, which is proper among Christians. It is an all-embracing love between family members that is also appropriate in the church. The use of *brother* with reference to the adherence of the same religion was, of course, not particular to Christians in the ancient world. It was common also to Jews and other religious communities in Egypt. To "be devoted to one another in brotherly love" was to regard other members of the Body of Christ as you would your immediate family. The same concern and protection you would extend, and the same sacrifice that you would make, to your own father, mother, or sibling is now commanded as "the norm" for all Christ-followers in their relationships with one another.

Although it was a big step of faith for Theresa and me with Pat, God did more than pay her rent and "wow" us with His power. A bond developed between us and her that we'd never experienced before. Jesus said, "Where ever your treasure is, your heart will be also." And this one act of placing our treasure toward meeting Pat's need created a new depth of authentic community. Without knowing it, we were obeying the two commands of Romans 12:10. Until we understand the importance of devotion as a core component to building authentic community, we will see our faith and relationships as merely a "nice club" or social group. The early church took quite seriously this command "to be devoted" to one another—at times at the cost of its brothers' own lives.

Merle: A Picture of Devotion

Perhaps a nonspiritual picture of devotion will help you grasp the intensity of this command. It is what I observed nearly every night as a freshman in college. I roomed with a wrestler who later became an all-American. He was a picture of devotion. Merle wore a plastic suit at night in order to sweat and lose weight. Before he went to bed, he got out a deck of cards and put the cards right in the center of the floor. Then he'd pull a small wheel with handles on it from under his bed and flip over a card. Whatever the card said with regard to the number, he did that many repetitions with his wheel, pulling it out in front of him to develop his abdominal and chest muscles. If it was a face card, it meant ten repetitions. All other cards were their face value. I would literally watch him go through an entire deck of cards before he went to bed. It made me hurt just watching him. Afterward, he'd take the deck of cards and go through the same process with the number of sit-ups. To say that Merle was devoted is an understatement. He was a picture of devotion; he didn't miss a night, and he was willing to pay a high price because his training really mattered to him.

Let me ask you: Is that how you think about serving others? Is that how you think about the Body of Christ? When you hear about a legitimate need in the life of a brother or sister, is that the kind of devotion you feel called to provide?

Can you imagine how "church" would change if this kind of devotion to one another was the normal way Christians treated fellow Christians? Or are we so busy there's no room in our hearts, no margin in our schedules to really love people that way? Has our faith become so organized and so structured around buildings and times and labels that the church is a place that we go to instead of something that we are? To be devoted to one another means we lay down our lives for one another.

When my father died, there's a reason why I got to have that meaningful conversation with him. I have a brother in Christ who is deeply devoted to me. Because of his work, he owns a private airplane that he flies around the country to check on his projects. In no uncertain terms, he told me, "Chip, when you hear about your dad, I want you to give me a call no matter what time it is and I will meet you ASAP at the airport and get you to North Carolina within an hour." When I got the call from the hospital, the first call I made was to Gary, and within thirty-five minutes, I was on his private jet heading toward North Carolina. The time didn't matter to him. The cost didn't matter to him. He was devoted to me. When we arrived there, I hardly noticed that Gary and his son had rented a car. They ushered me to the front door of the hospital that night and said, "Don't worry about where we'll stay tonight. We have everything taken care of."

Some of the most precious minutes I've ever spent with my father in my life were because I had a brother in Christ who didn't love me when it was convenient. He loved me when I needed it the most, at great personal cost. That's what it means to be devoted to one another. It is in that environment that authentic community thrives and bursts forth into life as the supernatural love of God is passed back and forth among God's children.

But devotion is only half the story. The second half of verse 10 says that we are to give preference to one another in honor. This is a passion for another person's success; it's literally "outdoing one another" in giving honor to another person. It's the idea of making the other person look good, to help them be successful, rather than focusing on yourself. This is what genuine humility looks like when it's played out in real life. Rather than competing for the limelight or "seeking to be number one," this passage unlocks God's means of developing unity in our relationships.

Steve: A Picture of Loyalty and Honor

One of the greatest seasons in my life was between my mid-thirties and late forties. For twelve and a half years, I had the privilege of being the senior pastor of the Santa Cruz Bible Church in California. It was a time of great personal and spiritual growth, the growth of my family, and the joy of working with a team of pastors who were among my closest and best friends. One of those pastors is a lifelong friend named Steve. Steve and I met during my early years in Texas, where he was a football coach, and we became fast friends. God later led him to go to seminary and into vocational ministry. Steve is one of the most multi-talented individuals I've ever met. He can teach, lead worship, lead a small group, solve the biggest problems, or figure out how to seize the greatest opportunities in an organization. Steve was my best friend and my right-hand man at Santa Cruz Bible Church for many years. He had the ability to take concepts and ideas and pull people together in the power of the Holy Spirit to make those ideas reality.

When I look back on the years of growth and fruitful ministry in Santa Cruz, I believe a great measure of the credit belongs to Steve's incredible gifts, loyalty, and the hand of God upon his life. I share all this because most people don't know much about Steve because Steve, like few people I've ever met, was devoted to honor me above himself. He went out of his way to defer to me. There were times when something great would happen in my life and I honestly believe he was more excited about it than I was.

> It's amazing how much grace there is to go around when people honestly long for the success of others more than their own.

Are you that kind of person? Do you honor and give preference to others? It's amazing how much grace there is to go around when people, from the heart, honestly long for the success of others more than their own. It's counterintuitive and so unlike the world's values, but it is refreshing and invigorating when you experience it in relationships. Being devoted to one another and giving preference to one another is all about the *real you* showing up and meeting *real needs*.

Jesus: The Perfect Picture of Devotion and Honor

The most profound picture of real needs being met out of humility and devotion is the cross. Jesus was devoted to you and me to the point of sacrificing Himself in our place to meet our biggest need—the forgiveness of our sins.

> *Who, being in very nature God, did not consider equality with God something to be grasped, but made himself nothing, taking the very nature of a servant, being made in human likeness. And being found in appearance as a man, he humbled himself and became obedient to death—even death on a cross!*
>
> —PHILIPPIANS 2:6–8 NIV

The cross is the greatest example of humility and devotion in the universe. Jesus put your needs ahead of His own. He considered you more valuable than Himself. So what might it look like for you to follow His example?

IT'S YOUR MOVE—Become an ⊙12 Christian

What are some real needs of the people in your relational network? What initiative could you take to meet some *real needs* in your community, your church, your small group, or in your family? Where did God speak to you about being devoted to someone or giving honor to someone? As we shared in the beginning of this chapter, the price is high, but the rewards are immeasurable.

THINK—What hit home with you in this chapter?

REFLECT—Who comes to mind when you think of someone who has *honored* you and been *devoted* to you? How do you feel about them?

UNDERSTAND—What person or situation are you aware of that would qualify as a *real* need? Who is hurting who needs help?

SURRENDER—You may not be the one to meet the need that you listed above; but tell God you are willing to make a real sacrifice to meet that need if that is His will.

TAKE ACTION—Get out of your comfort zone and convenient zone this week. Help one person in a way that "really costs you something."

MOTIVATION—Download the full-length audio message *How to Experience Authentic Community* at **Livingonthe Edge.org/r12.**

ENCOURAGE SOMEONE—Who has met a real need in your life in the past? Whether it was loaning you money, telling you the truth, helping heal your marriage, or driving your kids to practice . . . let them know how grateful you are to Christ for them.

.

CHAPTER NINETEEN

What's keeping you from experiencing authentic community?

*How can you believe if you accept praise from one another,
yet make no effort to obtain the praise
that comes from the only God?*[1]
—*Jesus of Nazareth*

Why do we want it so much and experience it so little? Why has church become an event that we attend rather than a community that we belong to? Why is it that even when we really get involved in ministry, it starts to feel a lot more like a duty to fulfill than serving people we love? Why do so many groups start well, but fizzle into something more social than spiritual, more superficial than transformational?

I began to learn the answer to these questions when I received a handwritten note on the back of a 3x5 card during the summer of 1975. I was attending a summer training program with a parachurch organization in Columbus, Ohio. We all gathered from our various colleges to take the next step toward in-depth spiritual growth and maturity. Within the first week, we all found jobs and lived in a large fraternity house just off the Ohio State campus.

The girls lived on one side of the house and the boys on the other.

We had Bible studies nightly, evangelism weekly, and each person was assigned to a team of four people with a team leader. My team leader's name was John, and he was a few years further down the road spiritually from me. Although it took me a long time to get going spiritually, I had turned the corner and was zealous to grow in every aspect of the Christian life.

I was memorizing Scripture like crazy, meeting with God every morning, praying through a prayer list on a daily basis, and looking for opportunities to share my faith with anyone who would listen. The group I was involved in had a pretty structured approach to the spiritual life; and the more goals and challenges they gave me, the more I stepped up to the plate to demonstrate that my passion was genuine . . . and suddenly I was "just a cut above the rest."

Whatever was asked of me, I did that summer. I had the right answers to the right questions and felt that at the end of the summer, I had distinguished myself as a next-generation leader in this Christian organization. At the end of the summer, we had an opportunity to meet individually with our team leader, who gave us his assessment of our spiritual growth and areas he felt we should consider working on as we headed back to our college campuses.

John was quiet and understated in his approach to leadership. I was honestly looking forward to the meeting, as I secretly hoped he had noticed the discipline I had modeled for the other members of my team, the servanthood that I had demonstrated in our relationships, and the knowledge and faith that were rapidly developing in my life. I had worked hard and was ready for a good pat on the back.

Our meeting didn't go quite the way I expected. Although I was full of zeal and had performed well throughout the summer, John's evaluation stunned me. His assessment of my spiritual growth was far different from my own. With very few words, he said he appreciated getting to know me throughout the summer and that God had revealed three verses to him to pass on to me. He encouraged me to consider meditating on them in preparation for the fall semester since I would be a part of the leadership team on our campus.

John handed me the 3x5 card with three handwritten verses:

For am I now seeking the favor of men, or of God? Or am I striving to please men? If I were still trying to please men, I would not be a bond-servant of Christ.

—GALATIANS 1:10 NASB

How can you believe, when you receive glory from one another and you do not seek the glory that is from the one and only God?

—JOHN 5:44 NASB

And He said to them, "You are those who justify yourselves in the sight of men, but God knows your hearts; for that which is highly esteemed among men is detestable in the sight of God."

—LUKE 16:15 NASB

After handing me the card, he asked me to read the verses silently. When I finished, he prayed that God would perform a significant work in my life in the coming fall. The meeting was very short and it didn't take a rocket scientist to figure out that there was a message here for me.

In Galatians 1:10, Paul says, he was not trying to please men. In John 5:44, Jesus essentially says, "It's impossible to genuinely trust Christ when you're seeking to please people." And when my eyes scanned Luke 16:15, a spiritual dagger went through my heart as I read "that which is highly esteemed among men is detestable in the sight of God."

You see, John had astutely observed that my performance and religious activity were geared not so much to please God or love other people as they were to gain approval and acceptance from my peers. I was well on my way to becoming a Pharisee, using the cloak of religion to further my own personal agenda by appearing spiritual, knowledgeable, and faithful.

As I walked slowly down the hall after that meeting and reread the verses on the 3x5 card, it felt like someone had punched me in the stomach when I wasn't ready. Levels of denial and pride rushed to the surface along with a deep sense of disappointment and sadness. As I stood motionless in that hallway I began to realize I really wasn't who I thought I was. Looking back, I can now see that my relationships in that training program weren't very deep or authentic, but more about impressing others and manipulating conversations to glorify *my* name and *my* reputation instead of God's.

I'd like to say that I read those three verses, committed them to memory, and solved that people-pleasing problem in my life, but I can't. I have battled being a people pleaser my whole life; and although I've made significant progress by the grace of God, it is a battle that I continue to fight to this day. But what I want you to see is that the turning point came in my life when someone had the opportunity and courage to address the "blind spots" in my life.

In Romans 12:11–13, the Apostle Paul continues to voice God's directives for experiencing authentic community. In the outline below, we are reminded that authentic community can only happen when the real you meets real needs. Now we will learn that hypocrisy not only occurs in our actions, but far more frequently in our motives.

In verse 11, the Apostle Paul gives us three pithy admonishments that deal specifically with our motives in going about meeting the real needs of one another.

Authentic Community Occurs When . . .

- the real you (v. 9) . . .
- meets real needs (v. 10) . . .
- for the right reason (v. 11) . . .
- in the right way (vv. 12–13).

THE *REAL* YOU—(V. 9)

- *Authenticity*—"Let love be sincere."
- *Purity*—"Hate what is evil. Cling to what is good."

MEETS *REAL* NEEDS—(V. 10)

- *Devotion*—"Be devoted to one another in brotherly love."
- *Humility*—"Giving preference to one another in honor."

FOR THE *RIGHT* REASON—(V. 11)

- *Motive*—**"Not lagging behind in diligence, fervent in spirit, serving the Lord."**
- *Method*—**"Genuine service to God is characterized by":**
  - *Diligence*—**excellence**
  - *Enthusiasm*—**passion**

IN THE *RIGHT* WAY—(VV. 12-13)

- *Upward Focus*—"Rejoicing in hope, persevering in tribulation, devoted to prayer."
- *Outward Focus*—"Contributing to the needs of the saints, practicing (pursuing) hospitality."

In these three brief admonitions God makes it clear that our service and relationships to one another need to be characterized by the right motive and the right method.

The Cost of Authentic Community

This first phrase is actually a harsh warning. The literal meaning of "not lagging behind in diligence" is "Don't be slothful!" or "Don't be slow or delay in doing something." People don't tend to use the word *sloth* anymore, yet the Bible speaks in very strong terms about the issue of slothfulness or laziness. According to Scripture, laziness is a sin. The book of Proverbs in particular speaks multiple times about the dire consequences of slothful behavior (Proverbs 24:30–34). But let me ask you something: When was the last time you ever heard someone reprove someone else for being lazy?

When was the last time you were in a small group study or in a mentoring relationship and someone said to you, "You know, Bob, I can see God is really working in your life, but you have a real problem in an area that I think he wants to address. You are very lazy." In our American Christian culture, calling someone lazy is the height of insult.

Laziness is the failure to do what needs to be done when it needs to be done.

It's just a place that we don't go. That's partly because it has cultural taboos, but also because we do not understand what the Bible is forbidding when it warns against laziness. Slothfulness or laziness is not watching old reruns of television all day as you sit on the couch and eat chocolate bonbons. Laziness is the failure to do what needs to be done when it needs to be done.

That's the classic definition of slothfulness or laziness. It's not that you're not busy or active; it's that you are not doing what needs to be done when it needs to be done. What God is saying here in Romans 12:11 is that when He prompts you to do something in your relationships with other believers, you need to do what needs to be done when it needs to be done.

The Fuel of Authentic Community

Closely related to this issue of slothfulness is the issue of passion or enthusiasm. This phrase *fervent in spirit* is literally a picture of water coming to the point of boiling. Our service for God in relationship to one another is to flow out of the passion we have in our own personal intimacy with Christ. We are to serve *Christ* with enthusiasm! We are to serve and love *one another* with zeal. One of the greatest enemies of authentic community is our own spirituality and religiosity.

In every group, in every church, in every Christian organization, there is a downward drag and propensity to begin to go through the motions. If we're not careful, we begin to do the right things without any heart or any passion. What used to be "delight" becomes duty. What used to be a genuine expression of our gratitude and love for God becomes something on our to-do list that we simply need to get done.

Our tithe and giving turns into paying one more bill. Our preparation for teaching God's word moves from the awesome joy in declaring the very words of the living God to glancing at a couple commentaries or a denominational quarterly on Saturday night to lay out a ho-hum lesson for your class or small group on Sunday morning. But why?! How does this happen, and how can we restore both excellence and passion to the way that we serve and care for one another?

I believe the answer is found in the very last phrase of Romans 12:11, *serving the Lord*. Do you realize how easy it is in our relationships to do things in the name of God, but it subtly becomes about serving *ourselves*? Like me and my summer program, you begin to "serve other people and do the right thing" because you get strokes for it. You get approval for it; you gain the admiration of people in your relationship network.

So often authentic community does not happen because people's motives are not focused on serving God but on using the Christian community as a means to heal personal wounds of the past and gain affirmation. In some groups, the false motive is more blatant and has shifted from serving God to financial gain. This theology has been floating around for some time that teaches that if you will give so much of your time and money to God, God is obligated to provide a prosperous financial return on your "spiritual investment." This is simply wrong.

Instead of serving God, the worship service becomes a "winning formula" to get something from God. We all struggle with our motives and to some degree I think we always will, but being sensitive to *why* we do what we do in serving one another in the Body of Christ is absolutely crucial.

How to Check Your Motives

When you are serving God for the right reason, you will do it with excellence and with passion. When you become more consciously aware that exercising your gifts to the building up of the Body of Christ is for the One who died for you, the One who's forgiven all your sins, the One who gave you life, and the One who's prepared a place for you in heaven, it will change how you serve. It will change the quality, the depth, and the sincerity of your service to others.

I think God in His kindness allows us to get a glimpse of our motives now and then, just to help us keep things in perspective. I am sure some of you reading the last couple of pages are asking yourself, *How do I know if my motives are pure or not?* The acid test for knowing whether you're serving God or serving yourself for the approval of others is how you respond when you're treated like a servant. How do you respond when you

> The acid test for knowing whether you're serving God or serving yourself for the approval of others is how you respond when you're treated like a servant.

don't get the "thank you"? How do you respond when you feel taken for granted and like no one notices what you're doing? How do you respond when your sacrifice and generosity are completely ignored?

The biggest test in my life have come when I have gone the extra mile to love and serve another person, and then been completely overlooked. How I respond in those situations causes me to evaluate why I do what I do. I remember one occasion when a church had an emergency situation and needed a speaker at the last moment. It was a very large church with a few hundred men gathered for a men's retreat with no speaker. Something had happened. Their original speaker had to cancel because of an emergency, and I was asked if there was any way I could help out. I prayed about it and got the "green" light from God to teach and a clear sense of what God wanted these men to hear. So along with the four weekend services that I would preach at our local church, I traveled out of town to minister to this group of men.

Once I got there, I was informed that there was a significant leadership issue among the staff and was asked if I would be willing to spend a couple hours in consultation with their leaders and later with one particular staff member. Again, I sensed God wanted me to help, and so I agreed. By Sunday morning, I was absolutely exhausted. I had spoken four times between Friday night and Saturday night, and been involved in meetings all throughout the day.

At the end of the retreat, as I headed home to prepare for my weekend services, one of the church leaders walked up to me, handed me an envelope, and said, "Thank you so much, brother. The Lord has used you in amazing ways here. This is just a little something for your time and service to us. We only wish it could be more."

I nodded in appreciation, got in the car, and drove home. I was absolutely wiped out, and had just put up my feet to look over my messages for the following day when the envelope I had been given dropped out of my Bible. I opened the envelope, and in it was a check. The size of the check shocked me. Not because it was large and generous, but because it was the smallest honorarium that I'd ever received.

This was a very large church with hundreds of men at the conference. And although I did not expect anything, and never demand a fee, this was an all-time low. In fact, I couldn't help myself, I figured out how many hours I had spent in the last day and a half and divided it by the amount of money they had given me and figured I didn't quite make minimum wage. A small resentment began to grow in my heart as I shook my head in disbelief.

I then began to think of the big day that I had tomorrow and why in the world did I spend the last thirty-six hours with this group? I mean, how ungrateful could they be! As I stuck the little check back in my Bible, the Spirit of God gently brought to my mind Galatians 1:10 and John 5:44. If I were still seeking to please men, I would not be a bond-servant of Christ.

"Chip," I heard the Spirit say, "why did you go and teach my Holy Word to those men? Did you do it to serve me or to please you?" In that moment I realized it really wasn't the size of the check that irritated me. It was that I wasn't appreciated, I wasn't valued, and I was simply treated like a servant. I asked God to forgive me for my attitude and thanked Him for the awesome privilege of teaching His Word and counseling those brothers in Christ.

If you really want to see your motives, just check your response when you're treated like a servant. It's a good test. For many years I have made it a practice never to look at a honorarium check until after I was through speaking so that what people do or don't do would never have an impact on what I do.

Authentic community happens when the *real you* meets *real needs* for the *right reason*. Loving people isn't about having ooey-gooey feelings or just doing it when you feel like it. Loving people isn't about doing it so that you'll be affirmed and esteemed, and become the object of the praises of men. *Loving people for the right reasons means we give others what they need the most when they deserve it the least at great personal cost.*

That's the way Jesus loves you and me, and that's the kind of love that brings forth the supernatural, joy-filled, bubbling-over, Spirit-empowered community that thrills our hearts and satisfies our souls.

IT'S YOUR MOVE—Become an ⊙12 Christian

As you think about your relationship with other believers, ask yourself where has God spoken to you about your motives? About your methods? Are you doing what needs to be done *when* it needs to be done as an act of service to Jesus Christ? And is that service growing out of your own intimate "bubbling-over" fervor and spirit relationship with Him, or do you find yourself stuck in the doldrums of religious activity and fulfilling obligations?

I want you to know it doesn't have to stay that way, and God longs for you to both give and receive authentic community. In the next chapter, we'll talk about some specific ways to break out of the patterns and cycles that keep us from experiencing and giving God's love to one another.

THINK—What story in this chapter did you relate to the most? Why?

REFLECT—How would you characterize your current service to God? Why?

- On fire
- Fading
- In need of passion

UNDERSTAND—What practical ways have helped you keep your service to God characterized by excellence and passion? What do you do when you are concerned about having improper motives?

SURRENDER—Ask God to help you see *your motives* through His eyes. Leisurely remember it's about loving God, not fulfilling people's expectations. Confess or rejoice as necessary.

TAKE ACTION—Take a long slow, walk and evaluate your present ministry involvement:

- Too much
- Too little
- None at all

MOTIVATION—Get the joy and adventure back in serving. Consider doing three acts of kindness this week. Buy coffee for the next person in line, get a meal for a homeless person, or meet a need secretly at work.

ENCOURAGE SOMEONE—If you apply this verse, "Not lagging behind in diligence, fervent in spirit, serving the Lord" (Romans 12:10), you will encourage many!

•

CHAPTER TWENTY

Where's your focus?

My prayer is not for them alone. I pray also for those
who will believe in me through their message,
that all of them may be one, Father,
just as you are in me and I am in you.
May they also be in us so that the world
may believe that you have sent me.[1]
—*Jesus of Nazareth*

The young man sitting on the couch was strong and handsome. He'd been an all-state wrestler in high school and landed a premier head-coaching job despite his being barely over a quarter of a century old. But tonight, this strong, macho, "never give up" wrestling coach is crying profusely in front of nine or ten brothers and sisters in Christ. His father died several weeks earlier and family wrangling over "stuff" was breaking his heart. As he wept, we cried out to God on his behalf. There was no embarrassment, only acceptance. When he regained his composure, he blurted out words that cemented us as a group, "Thank you, guys, for being here for me, I needed to be here so badly tonight."

As we all prepared to leave for the evening, I noticed the hugs were a little longer. The bonds were a little stronger and the presence of God seemed to linger even after everyone was gone.

Love is giving another person what they need the most when they deserve it the least at great personal cost. On this particular night a young man experienced Jesus' love for him through the lives of His followers.

Love grows in "community." It is an overwhelming need in our culture. What we need more than anything else in our connection to one another is love. Not just social connection or being nice to one another, but love. It's love that never fails. It's love that doesn't give up. It's love that helps people through the worst of times. It's love that sent Jesus to the earth and later to the cross.

It's love that conquers fear, heals wounds, and restores broken relationships. But love is hard. In fact, there are many times when I know what love looks like, but I just don't want to give it. What do you do when you know what it means to love someone but everything in you screams, "I just can't do it! I don't have anything to give"?

Love is giving another person what they need the most when they deserve it the least at great personal cost.

God's Word is not only true, but it is amazingly practical. God understands our struggle to love. God understands our struggle to be holy. God understands that authentic community occurs not only when the *real me* meets *real needs* for the *right reason,* but that it has to happen in the *right way.* Meeting others' needs in the right way is often very difficult, so He gives us hope by showing us how to find strength and power when we have none of our own.

The hope is found in this final section about how to experience authentic community; and notice how each portion of this passage builds on the other.

Authentic Community Occurs When . . .

- the real you (v. 9) . . .
- meets real needs (v. 10) . . .
- for the right reason (v. 11) . . .
- in the right way (vv. 12–13).

THE REAL YOU—(V. 9)

- *Authenticity*—"Let love be sincere."
- *Purity*—"Hate what is evil. Cling to what is good."

MEETS REAL NEEDS—(V. 10)

- *Devotion*—"Be devoted to one another in brotherly love."
- *Humility*—"Giving preference to one another in honor."

FOR THE RIGHT REASON—(V. 11)

- *Motive*—"Not lagging behind in diligence, fervent in spirit, serving the Lord."
- *Method*—"Genuine service to God is characterized by":
  - *Diligence*—excellence
  - *Enthusiasm*—passion

IN THE RIGHT WAY—(VV. 12-13)

- **Upward Focus—"Rejoicing in hope, persevering in tribulation, devoted to prayer."**
- **Outward Focus—"Contributing to the needs of the saints, practicing (pursuing) hospitality."**

Someone has said, "Your outlook will determine your outcome," and I believe that's true. When I feel tired, overwhelmed, and underappreciated, my focus quickly turns inward. I begin to think about what I don't have and who has not been coming through for me. I begin to focus on prayers that have not been answered and relationships that are troubling.

My mind unconsciously drifts to what I don't like about my circumstances, wishing things were better, and I quickly lose perspective. My inward focus usually launches a mini–pity party for Chip Ingram—where I whine, complain, and grumble to God and to a few close friends. "Life's not fair, and the future seems beyond what I can endure." I'm sure everyone goes through these times—I'm convinced brief periods of inward focus are just a part of being human and growing in our relationship with Christ.

But an inward focus over a long period of time can produce discouragement and even depression. An inward focus will gradually lead to bad theology and a set of unrealistic expectations that make us the kind of people who give up on God, ourselves, and others. In this section, God reminds us that authentic community demands more than authenticity and purity. It demands more than devotion and humility. And it even demands more than diligence and enthusiasm as we seek to serve God in our relationship with others. Authentic community demands an upward and outward focus. It demands an upward focus because authentic community is always built in the midst of opposition. The world, the flesh, and the enemy work in concert to destroy deep, authentic, loving relationships among God's children.

Authentic community demands an upward and outward focus.

Think about it. If the most powerful apologetic in the world is Christians loving Christians and Christians living like Christians, then doesn't it make sense that the enemy and the world system will be targeted specifically to destroy authentic community? And if that's the case, then it's only natural that God would provide us with clear instruction about how to overcome an inward and downward focus.

When I use the phrase *in the right way,* I mean this in contrast to attempting to build authentic community in the wrong way. The right way is out of the supernatural power of Christ. The wrong way is attempting to build authentic community out of the power of our own self-effort, personality, and the strength of the flesh.

I hope you realize that much of what we've talked about in authentic community is not merely difficult for you to do: it is impossible. You do not have the power to love others, to give to others what they need the most when they deserve it the least at great personal cost. And so, in verse 12, Paul gives us three brief phrases that instruct us about how to draw on the supernatural power of the Holy Spirit to maintain an upward focus.

Developing an Upward Focus

The first phrase, *rejoicing in hope*, refers to a mind-set. The second phrase, *persevering in tribulation*, is an action, and the third phrase, *devoted to prayer*, is a resource. What does it mean to rejoice in hope? To understand that phrase, we need to be careful not to insert the way we typically use the word *hope*, into the biblical text.

In English, the word *hope* primarily means wishful thinking. "I hope it doesn't rain tomorrow." "I hope the stock market goes up." "I hope things get better at work." These are statements of desire or wishful thinking, but the word *hope*, as used in the Bible, is not a reference to wishful thinking, but to an object of trust because we can know something with absolute certainty. The Scripture talks about the return of Christ as our blessed *hope*.

It is the certainty of His return that Paul references six or seven times in the book of 1 Thessalonians to encourage believers to continue in the faith, to love one another, and to persevere in suffering and adversity. As Americans, we tend to rejoice or find our joy and happiness in the fulfillment of circumstances. In fact, the word *happiness* has to do with happenings or things that happen. So, we are happy when good things are happening, and unhappy when circumstances change.

By contrast, joy is unaffected by circumstances and is rooted in hope. Things may be difficult and circumstances may be tough, but our hope does not change. We are forgiven children of God who are sealed by the Spirit of God and adopted into the family of God with a place reserved for us in heaven for all eternity. This is our hope! Paul says an upward focus is a mind-set whereby we live in light of eternity.

In the face of injustice, illness, financial loss, and global and economic uncertainties, we have hope. And this hope leads to a very clear and specific action. In Romans 12:12, we're told to "persevere in tribulation." *Persevere* is an interesting word, used multiple times in the New Testament. It's a compound word: *hupo meno*. *Hupo* means "to be under," and *meno* means "to be under stress, difficulty, or adversity." It's a word picture of the weight of the world being carried on your back.

We are commanded to hold up under stress and pressure in the midst of tribulation or difficulty. God promises that He will actually use the hardship for our good. James puts it this way:

> Consider it all joy, my brethren, when you encounter various trials, knowing that the testing of your faith produces endurance. And let endurance have its perfect result, so that you may be perfect and complete, lacking in nothing.
>
> JAMES 1:2–4 NASB

As you build relationships in the Body of Christ, difficult things happen. Our natural inclination is to focus inward and to blame God or to blame others. But Scripture says, "Don't give up, don't give in, and don't bail out." It is in persevering through the difficulties that our characters are developed (Romans 5:1–5), and through these difficulties that our deepest relationships are forged.

When I look back on my closest friends, they aren't the people I necessarily had the most fun with, but those who have been with me through the most difficult times of my life. Think of who you are closest to in your life. I would guess that it's those people who were there for you during the pain of a failing marriage, a troubled child, a positive biopsy report, a bankruptcy, or a false accusation. It is in these times that we let down the walls of protection and open our hearts and bare our soul with those few trusted people who are willing to go through life's deepest valleys with us.

Authentic community is not for the faint of heart. We must take off our masks, walk in purity, and enter one another's lives with devotion and sacrifice. All the superficial desires to impress fade away as you shed tears together in the ICU, in hopes that your mate or one of your children will live through the surgery. Authentic community is far more than having a small group meet in your living room and talk about biblical passages.

Authentic community is facing life's most painful trials together while finding your hope in Christ and His promises. But how does it work? How do you get the strength to face the impossible and care for one another when your strength is gone? The answer is three little words . . . "devoted to prayer."

This last phrase, *devoted to prayer,* is a strong one. Just as we are devoted to one another, an upward focus demands that we seek supernatural strength and resources to help one another. "Devoted to prayer" is a picture of people who go before the throne of God regularly and passionately to ask God to do in the lives of one another what no human power can ever accomplish.

I have probably met only a handful of people in all my life whom I could actually describe as "devoted to prayer." My wife is one of them. I have watched her spend hours in tears before the face of God on my behalf, my children's, and for the people God has brought into our lives. I have learned from her and from others like her that a connection from the heart with others happens far more quickly and authentically on your knees than it does in hours of discussion about the affairs of the day.

If you want to take your group, your family, or your church to the next level, let me encourage you to ask God to show you what it looks like to be devoted to prayer for one another and in your time with one another. If you desire to cultivate and develop your prayer experience, I recommend *The Power of Prayer* by R. A. Torrey or an audio series I did by the same title.

In the last few chapters we have studied God's prescription for authentic community. We have learned that the beauty of relational connectedness requires us to:

1. Take off our masks and be pure.
2. Be devoted to one another and honor one another above ourselves.
3. Serve God with passion and excellence.
4. Carry one another's burdens in the midst of difficulty.

When God's children begin to relate to one another in this way, some very exciting things happen—the level of love in relationships blossoms. People become open and vulnerable with one another. People learn to agree to disagree on the minor issues, and begin to love one another around the major ones. And into this rich relational setting, we are reminded of our need for an outward focus.

Developing an Outward Focus

There is a very real danger that we will begin to love with words and emotions instead of with deeds and truth. It's easy to fall into the trap of thinking we really love one another because we provide emotional support, pray with one another, and demonstrate verbal concern. The command to "contribute to the needs of the saints" moves authentic community beyond the realm of small group discussion and to the place where the rubber meets the road.

Authentic community demands that your wallet must come out of your pocket. You must give financially, sacrificially, and systematically to those who have needs in the Body of Christ. I am not talking about your tithe or systematic giving to your church in this context, but to the needs of brothers and sisters in your relational network. As much as I appreciate our government's tax deductions for charitable giving, we have lost sight of extending compassion and meeting practical needs for one another when a deduction is not involved. We are a body. Our money is not our own; our houses are not our own; our cars are not our own; our stuff is not our own—it's God's.

It's all on loan and we're simply stewards. He can tap us on the shoulder at any time to reallocate the funds entrusted to us to meet the needs of other people. The Apostle James admonished the early church not to love simply in word and tongue, but also in deed and truth:

> What use is it, my brethren, if someone says he has faith but he has no works? Can that faith save him? If a brother or sister is without clothing and in need of daily food, and one of you says to them, "Go in peace, be warmed and be filled," and yet you do not give them what is necessary for their body, what use is that? Even so faith, if it has no works, is dead, being by itself.
>
> —JAMES 2:14–17 NASB

I believe the early church members lived in an authentic community with one another, and as legitimate needs surfaced among them, they simply reached into their pockets and provided financial assistance with the wisdom and discernment that the Spirit provided. It's a powerful and beautiful thing when, at a grassroots level, people begin to reach out and meet one another's needs.

This kind of authentic community happened during our Monday-night Bible study with a group of young professionals. As we sat around Theresa's and my living room, a freelance photographer shared his dreams and the mission that God had placed on his heart. He was taking huge steps of faith to follow what God had called him to do and it was creating significant financial tension. There were other needs in the group as well, so we closed our time with prayer and interceding for one another.

Two days later, our freelance photographer told me that when he went out to his car after Bible study, there was an envelope taped to his windshield with two hundred-dollar bills in it. The look on his face could have lit up the room, as he was in awe of God's love. He could hardly grasp that someone in our group had heard about his need and anonymously wanted to "contribute to the needs of a saint" (him). It's this life-on-life radical caring for one another that causes the world to stop and take notice.

If you've ever had the experience of being in a group like this, you know what I'm talking about. The time when the group gathers becomes an oasis of life and encouragement. For me, Monday night is the highlight of my week. Authentic community can actually get so good that we are in danger of turning our collective focus inward instead of maintaining an outward focus. And so immediately after we are commanded to "contribute to the needs of the saints," we are urged to "practice hospitality." Literally, "pursuing strangers." Opening our lives and our group to those who are lonely, isolated, or in need is a part of how we do life with one another. The danger as we develop close-knit relationships with one another happens when we begin to develop that "us four and no more" mentality.

Can you think of someone in your church or in your neighborhood who doesn't fit in? Who needs a hand? Who needs some love? What could you, as a group, do to reach beyond the scope of your own personal needs to help someone who is a stranger? Who needs to share a meal with you? Who needs to "feel that he belongs" and feel cared for by you, your family, or your small group?

When the world sees God's people step up and love those who are unlike them, and especially those who are unlovely, it takes notice. When black and white, Asian, Indian, and Hispanic people really love one another and genuinely care to the point of sacrifice, that's when the world begins to recognize that God is at work. When Democrats, Republicans, and independents put aside their differences and say that the flag that will fly over their relationships is Jesus—not politics— then walls come tumbling down and grace comes rolling in.

On the last night that Jesus walked upon the earth, He gave a new command to those He loved the most—that **they would love one an-**

other in the same way that He had loved them. Jesus then prayed for His followers who were with Him, and for all of us who would believe through them, that we would *become one* even as the Father and the Son are one, and that we would love one another in such a way that the world would know that God sent Jesus to be the Savior of all mankind.

IT'S YOUR MOVE—Become an ⊙12 Christian

Authentic community is the most powerful apologetic on the face of the earth. It's the greatest need among Christians, and the greatest need for an unbelieving world to begin to believe that what we say about Jesus is true because of how we love and relate to one another. Authentic community is rare and powerful, but it *can* and *will* happen when the *real you* meets *real needs* for the *right reason* in the *right way*.

Let's stop going to church; let's be the church!

THINK—What was most encouraging in this chapter to you? Why?

REFLECT—What was most convicting in this chapter? Why?

UNDERSTAND—In what specific circumstance do you need an upward focus? Who could you talk with to process this challenge in your life?

SURRENDER—Are you currently experiencing authentic community as defined in Romans 12:9–13? Are you willing to take whatever step necessary to rearrange your schedule and take initiative to build the kind of relationships that "SHOUT TO THE WORLD" that Jesus is the Son of God?

TAKE ACTION—Do whatever you need to do to obey John 13:34–35 to receive the love God wants you to have. Get off the sidelines. Get connected.

MOTIVATION—Consider joining a small group if you are not presently in one or invite a friend you know is hurting to the group you attend.

ENCOURAGE SOMEONE—Consider sending the r12 link to someone at another church or in another city to encourage them toward spiritual maturity. Go to **LivingontheEdge.org/r12.**

B.I.O.
(BEFORE GOD DAILY, IN COMMUNITY WEEKLY, ON MISSION 24/7)

B.I.O. is the pathway to becoming an R12 disciple.

BEFORE GOD DAILY

Serving in love and experiencing authentic community isn't just relationally horizontal. There is a vertical component to community that often gets overlooked. In Romans 12:12, right in the middle of this passage about serving in love, Paul calls on us to be "devoted to prayer." We are regularly and passionately to go before the throne of God to intercede for others.

Coming before God daily is not just about opening your Bible and getting to know God better. It is also a great opportunity to come before our God and gracious Father and bring the needs of our friends. One of the most powerful ways you support those in your small group is by praying for them. In the next week, ask a friend or two how you can pray specifically for them. Then carry those prayer requests to God as you come before Him.

IN COMMUNITY WEEKLY

As I wrote earlier in this section "the most powerful apologetic in the world is Christians loving Christians." The credibility of our faith rises or falls on how well we model authentic, loving community.

The passages we studied in this section, Romans 12:9–13, provide a great portrait of what authentic community looks like. This kind of community is not for the faint of heart, and you will never simply drift into the kind of relationships described in Romans 12. We must take off our masks, walk in purity, pray for one another, and enter into one another's lives with devotion and sacrifice.

I believe small groups can be a great petri dish for learning how to live in true community. This kind of community takes time and intentionality. That's why we encourage you to be in community weekly.

So, are you currently experiencing the kinds of relationships described in Romans 12:9–13? Are you willing to take whatever step is necessary to rearrange your schedule and take the initiative to build relationships that shout to the world that Jesus is the Son of God?

ON MISSION 24/7

One of the dangers of community is that we can turn our focus completely inward. That's why it's important for us to heed Paul's challenge to contribute to the needs of the saints and practice hospitality (Romans 12:13 NIV). Literally, that means to "pursue strangers." This isn't a call for a church benevolence program. It is a call to everyday

Christians like you and me to meet the needs of people around us. Every week your life intersects that of someone in need. If you are going to be *On Mission*, you are going to have to get out of your comfort zone and convenience zone. Let it become your lifestyle that you follow the nudgings of the Holy Spirit to help those in need. As I challenged you in this section, help one person in a way that really costs you something. It might be fun to involve your whole group in helping.

How to Overcome the Evil Aimed at You

SUPERNATURALLY RESPONDING TO EVIL WITH GOOD

ROMANS 12:14-21

God is holy and He has made holiness the moral condition
necessary to the health of His Universe.
Sin's temporary presence in the world only accents this.
Whatever is holy is healthy;
evil is a moral sickness that must end ultimately in death.[1]

—*A. W. Tozer*

CHAPTER TWENTY-ONE

Who has hurt you the most?

You have heard that it was said,
"Love your neighbor and hate your enemy."
But I tell you: Love your enemies
and pray for those who persecute you . . .[2]
—*Jesus of Nazareth*

As we start this final section of this book, I would like you to think of the person in your life who has hurt you the most. This person may be someone who has treated you unfairly; it may be someone who has gossiped about you; it might even be someone in your younger years who abused you either physically, sexually, or emotionally.

For others, this person might be the one who walked out on you. Perhaps it was a father or a mother who simply walked out of your life, or maybe it's the person who you gave your heart to—never dreaming they would ever betray you. It might be someone you deeply trusted who later lied to you, stole your money, and wounded someone you loved, or attempted to actually ruin your life. We all have people from our past who have done evil to us. Our tendency is to bury the wounds and never fully deal with the damage or continue to live with a deep-seated bitterness toward them. Neither option represents God's will for our lives, but after counseling for over twenty years, I find that most people simply do not know how to respond to the evil aimed at them.

My prayer is that you will not skip over the penetrating questions in the above paragraph. As painful as they may be, I pray that you will vividly bring to mind the face of that person who has been the conduit of evil and pain in your life. God has a dream for your life and that dream involves every relationship that you experience on the earth—even the difficult ones. We've talked about what it looks like for an authentic follower in his/her relationship with God, the world, themselves, with believers, and now we need to examine carefully our relationship with those who are opposed to Christ and do evil to His followers.

How does an r12 Christian respond to their enemies? What does it look like to allow the Spirit of God to give us the grace to treat those who have unjustly wronged us the way Jesus would treat them? How do we deal with those people we have anger fantasies about in our mind, fantasies in which we play out their getting what they deserve and receiving the justice and due payment for what they've done to us?

I know of nothing more difficult in life than to deal with those people who have been the source of evil aimed at our lives. Whether it's abuse, injustice, financial loss, emotional betrayal, or physical beating; moving beyond our wounds, hate, and bitterness often seems impossible.

Unlike many who may read these words, I had a relatively positive childhood with parents who cared about me. I endured the small attacks that everyone goes through, but none of the major traumas that produce lifelong wounds or feelings of hatred toward another person. That changed, however, my freshman year of college.

My Biggest Enemy

I played basketball in college and had a teammate named Jimmy (not his real name) who was much older than the rest of the players on the team. He was a Vietnam veteran who was about six-six or six-seven and had a vertical leap over forty inches. He was an amazing athlete and an accomplished artist. He landed at our small liberal arts college because the trauma and mistakes of his past disqualified him for a Division I school. He was in his late twenties and had spent time in prison for drug possession and dealing after being wounded in Vietnam. While he was very talented, Jimmy's nervous system was impaired from the war and drug use, so he had difficulty at times catching and handling the ball.

Jimmy came to college as a reformed drug addict and aspiring artist who was getting a second chance. He was very articulate and bright. Jimmy had seen and experienced a lot of evil in his life. He came from the inner city, served in the armed forces and was badly wounded in Vietnam, killed many people, and experienced the underbelly of society through drugs, illicit sex, and prison. He was very vocal and had an icy-cold stare that could send chills up your back. Jimmy described himself as "evil," and he wasn't kidding.

Somewhere along the way Jimmy discovered that I was a Christian. I was brand-new in Christ (perhaps six months) and earnestly seeking to live out my faith on the basketball team. Jimmy must have had some very negative experiences with Christians, as they were the object of his disdain and hatred. It wasn't long before I was the object of Jimmy's jokes and attacks. He publicly humiliated me in front of the entire team for my commitment to sexual purity prior to marriage. I was harassed and the object of locker-room dialogue that "sliced and diced me" from morning until night. He constantly referred to me as "Cheee-up, the skinny white boy who is a virgin and believes in Jesus." He had a way of saying my name and elongating the vowels in a way that made it sound like a cussword. I played basketball in the inner city growing up to hone my game in high school, so the issue with Jimmy was not racial, it was spiritual. Every opportunity, every road trip, and every situation was fair game for Jimmy's condemnation and ridicule.

My hatred for Jimmy grew with each passing day. His attacks were relentless and our size differential made physically fighting him suicidal. So as a point guard who could handle the ball well (and probably a little too fancy at times), I repaid Jimmy's comments with behind-the-back passes as hard as I could that would slip through his hands and hit him in the face. The coach would then berate Jimmy for not being ready for the ball and the sense of satisfaction and revenge I felt was great. For months the battle raged with Jimmy's verbal attacks nonstop and my on-the-court "no-look" passes dishing out punishment on his less-than-responsive, damaged reflexes.

One day everything came to a head and took our semipetty conflict to a whole new level. As I was walking down the hallway to my room in the dorm, the door across the hall opened briefly. Inside, I saw Jimmy and a group of others smoking dope. The smoke filled the room and Jimmy caught my eye as I was preparing to enter my room. Since Jimmy had come to the school under the guise of a "reformed drug addict and dealer," being caught with drugs would violate his probation and send him back to the life he hated. Jimmy bolted out of the door and grabbed my arm, spinning me around, and pressed his hand against my neck. "Cheee-up, you tell anyone what you saw here today and I will kill you! I have killed plenty of men before and one more won't make much difference."

I was scared to death. The look in his eyes and the intensity of his words made it clear that these were no idle threats. My dislike and disdain for Jimmy's harassment turned into pure, unadulterated hatred.

Hate is evil even when it is a response to injustice, wounds, or attack.

I had anger fantasies that I'm ashamed to share. I wanted to hurt Jimmy. I wanted to pay him back. I wanted him out of my life. And in a moment of weakness, under the right circumstances, I am certain I could have done something that I would be sorry for doing the rest of my life.

Hate is strong! It's evil even when it is a response to injustice, wounds, or attack. To hate evil is a good thing, but to hate people opens the door for evil to manifest its presence and grow in our own hearts. I was miserable and my stomach churned in knots. I was afraid and constantly looking over my shoulder, wondering if and when Jimmy might make good on his promise. I tried to play hardball on the court and looked for every opportunity to get back at Jimmy, but nothing worked. In desperation, I shared what had been going on and how I was feeling with another man named Jimmy who was helping lead the college ministry with whom I had become involved.

Serve My Worst Enemy! Are You Kidding?

Jimmy listened patiently. He asked a number of clarifying questions about the specifics of what had happened and how I was feeling. He then tilted his head and said, "Chip, I think this man is very evil. And there is only one thing I know of that is more powerful than this kind of evil, and that is the *good* that comes from God. Chip, I think I know what God wants you to do, but I want to warn you that even though I know it will work, it won't be easy." With that, Jimmy opened his Bible to Romans 12:14–21 and began reading out loud . . .

> Bless those who persecute you; bless and do not curse. Rejoice with those who rejoice; mourn with those who mourn.
>
> Live in harmony with one another. Do not be proud, but be willing to associate with people of low position. Do not be conceited.
>
> Do not repay anyone evil for evil. Be careful to do what is right in the eyes of everybody. If it is possible, as far as it depends on you, live at peace with everyone.
>
> Do not take revenge, my friends, but leave room for God's wrath, for it is written: "It is mine to avenge; I will repay," says the Lord. On the contrary:

"If your enemy is hungry, feed him;
if he is thirsty, give him something to drink.
In doing this, you will heap burning coals on his head."
Do not be overcome by evil, but overcome evil with good.

As Jimmy closed the Bible, a journey began that I will never forget. It was extraordinarily difficult to obey this passage; but I chose to do some things that made no sense, humanly speaking. I will share in detail exactly what God led me to do and how you can apply this to your life a little later. But first, God had to remove the bitterness from my heart and the hatred from my soul.

God freed me from the prison that I had made for myself and the poison of revenge that I was drinking. So let me ask you a couple of questions before we continue:

- Are you ready to learn how to deal with that person who's been the source and conduit of evil in your life?
- Are you willing to face some of the pain of your past and allow God to cleanse and heal you as you learn how to treat your enemies God's way by the power of the Holy Spirit?

IT'S YOUR MOVE—Become an Ω12 Christian

For some of you this is not an issue of the past; it concerns someone you work with, someone in your family, or someone with whom you share custody of your children. I want you to know that God has very specific instructions for his authentic followers about how to respond to the evil aimed at you. There is hope and there is help! We'll look at the first step in the next chapter.

THINK—What person came to your mind?

REFLECT—What emotions followed when this person came to your mind?

UNDERSTAND—In what ways have you sought to resolve this wound in the past? What's been helpful, or not helpful?

SURRENDER—Ask God to help you *be willing* to follow His commands in Romans 12:14–21 concerning this person.

TAKE ACTION—Identify one trusted friend you can share this old wound with and ask them to walk with you. As you do this, you will learn how to bless your enemies and it will free your soul.

MOTIVATION—Watch the fourteen-minute video message "How to Overcome the Evil Aimed at You" at r12 online (**LivingontheEdge.org/r12**) to get into greater depth on this passage.

ENCOURAGE SOMEONE—Offer to listen to someone who has been deeply wounded. Gently introduce Romans 12:14–21 to them.

CHAPTER TWENTY-TWO

Will you let Christ heal you?

For if you forgive men when they sin against you,
your heavenly Father will also forgive you.
But if you do not forgive men their sins,
your Father will not forgive your sins.[1]
—*Jesus of Nazareth*

As my friend opened the Bible and read aloud Romans 12:14–21, I listened quietly and I shook my head back and forth. The words did not make any sense to me. They certainly weren't anything that I wanted to do or thought would be of any help. Where is the justice? Where is the part where God swoops in and protects me and saves me from this evil man? What does it mean to bless those who persecute you, to bless and curse not? To be honest, I didn't want to curse Jimmy, I wanted to kill him.

Many of you may feel the same way right now. For others, this whole discussion may seem a lot like someone ripping a scab off an old wound. But let me assure you that God's solution is powerful and effective. When you begin to understand and act on this truth, you will experience firsthand the power of good for evil.

So let's take a look at this passage together and learn the first steps toward overcoming evil with good. I've written out this passage in a way that helps you see the structure and the meaning of the text:

Two Commands and a Warning

POSITIVE COMMAND (VV. 14-16)

Bless those who persecute you; bless and do not curse. Rejoice with those who rejoice, and weep with those who weep. Be of the same mind toward one another; do not be haughty in mind, but associate with the lowly. Do not be wise in your own estimation.

NEGATIVE COMMAND (VV. 17-20)

Never pay back evil for evil to anyone. Respect what is right in the sight of all men. If possible, so far as it depends on you, be at peace with all men. Never take your own revenge, beloved, but leave room for the wrath of God, for it is written, "VENGEANCE IS MINE, I WILL REPAY," says the Lord.

> *"But if your enemy is hungry, feed him, and if he is thirsty, give him a drink; for in so doing you will heap burning coals on his head."*

WARNING (V. 21)

Do not be overcome by evil, but overcome evil with good.

Notice that this passage is divided into two major commands—a positive command (verses 14–16) followed by a negative command (verses 17–20). Then verse 21 summarizes it all in the form of a final warning and application of this entire passage.

The positive command—*"Bless those who persecute you"*—is the overarching theme of the entire section. In verse 14, we will learn what it means to "bless and not curse." In verse 15, we will learn specifically how to bless those who've done evil to us. And in verse 16, we are warned to guard our perception of ourselves when we are dealing with evil people who do evil things. Under the right circumstances, we can also become the authors of evil in the lives of others if we are not careful. Evil has an amazing ability to latch on to even innocent parties, when our hurt and wounds cry out for "payback" and justice.

When my friend read this passage out loud, I didn't know what it meant. I don't use the word *bless* or *curse* very often, so I was unclear on what it meant to bless or curse someone. Since that time, I've done some research that will help us understand exactly what God is saying in this passage. "To bless" someone literally means to wish someone well, to desire God's favor and blessing upon their lives. By contrast, "to curse" means to pray against, to call down doom, to wish for their disaster, failure, and misfortune. This passage was commanding just the opposite of what I was doing. I was cursing the one who was persecuting me.

I have to admit (being a new Christian at that time) that this command made no sense to me at all. Why should I bless someone who had been so mean and unkind to me? Why should I care, let alone be kind to someone who verbally abused me, embarrassed me, and even threatened my life? How does this command "to bless" overcome evil, and why should I even consider doing it?

It was then that I was directed to the most radical words ever uttered on the face of the earth. They were uttered by a rabbi who is considered to be the greatest teacher of all time and by all accounts the greatest revolutionary in human history. And what he said to his first group of followers who were at the time being persecuted by the Roman government as well as by the religious leaders of their time stopped me in my tracks:

You have heard that it was said, "Love your neighbor and hate your enemy." But I tell you: Love your enemies and pray for those who persecute you, that you may be sons of your Father in heaven. He causes his sun to rise on the evil and the good, and sends rain on the righteous and the unrighteous. If you love those who love

*you, what reward will you get? Are not even the tax collectors do-
ing that? And if you greet only your brothers, what are you doing
more than others? Do not even pagans do that?*

Be perfect, *therefore, as your heavenly Father is perfect.*

—JESUS OF NAZARETH IN MATTHEW 5:43–48 NIV

It was then that I realized that the Apostle Paul was merely applying
for the church in Rome the very words of Jesus. Jesus taught His followers exactly how to respond to the evil aimed at them. And contrary
to the popular teaching of his day, Jesus gave radical instructions
that He would not only teach, but later model for them by dying for His
enemies on the cross—conquering evil, sin, and death once and for
all.

Jesus is calling us to respond to the evil aimed at us in the same way
that He did. Look at the two verbs in the passage above in Matthew
5:44—*love* your enemies, *pray* for those who persecute you, so that you
will be "sons of the Most High." "Sons of the Most High" translates a
Hebrew expression that denotes likeness. In other words, when we love
our enemies and pray for those who persecute us, we take on family
likeness. We mimic God and imitate the action of Jesus when we do to
our enemies what Jesus did to His. He solidifies this argument with the
next phrase, reminding us that God acts this way all the time. He
causes it to rain on both the evil and the good. Jesus then challenges
His followers and us today to live differently from the pagans and the
unbelievers, who befriend one another and love only those who love
them.

How Do We Really "Bless" Our Enemies?

But how does this work? What is the first step in blessing those who
have persecuted or are persecuting us? Inherent in the word *bless* is the
desire for the salvation of that person. No matter what they've done or

how badly they have hurt or abused us, we are commanded to bless them. This begins with an honest desire for God to forgive their sins. Before we can ever hope to love our enemies, we must start by willfully choosing to forgive them. We must forgive them in the same way that God has forgiven us. Jesus' final command in Matthew 5:48 is that we "be perfect" (the word means spiritually mature—it's the Greek word *teleos,* meaning to fulfill your God-given design) even as our heavenly Father is perfect.

To be quite honest, this is where many of us get stuck. The thought of forgiving the person who has done such evil against us seems repulsive and impossible. We confuse the *feeling* of forgiving with the *action* of forgiving someone. We unwisely and wrongly believe that to forgive someone is to "let them off the hook" and therefore justice will never be served. Someone has pointed out that those who refuse to forgive are like those drinking the poison of their own vengeance, hoping it will make the other person sick.[2]

But bitterness and hatred are like a cancer to our soul. When we refuse to forgive a person, the one we are hurting the most is ourselves. Yet no matter how many verses we hear about forgiveness or how many appeals are made to our logic, many of us simply refuse to let go of the wounds of the past by forgiving the one who inflicted them. I know, I've been there and I've done it! I believe much of our reluctance is rooted in a warped understanding of what it means to forgive someone and a lack of knowledge of exactly how to do it.

So let me explain to you what the Bible means when it says we are to forgive. Forgiveness is a three-stage process. Or for you language lovers out there, there are three verb forms of forgiveness.

- *Stage 1—"to forgive"—is a choice; an act of the will.* You do not need to feel like forgiving someone to do it. You do need to choose to release any desire for retribution and to ask God to treat the offending person in the same way God has treated you—with mercy.

- *Stage 2—"forgiving"—is a process whereby your choice to forgive begins over time to align with your emotions.* This process sometimes takes months or even years. On one particular occasion when I was severely betrayed, I chose to forgive the person in a deliberate act of will and wrote the date and time in my journal. However, a few days later I heard more information about this person's false accusations and my emotions began to spin out of control. I had already forgiven him of his sin, but this new information ripped off the scab of healing that had begun in my heart. There was no new sin, but the issue was brought again to my conscious mind and stirred up emotions of anger and bitterness.

This is where many Christians get caught in a vicious cycle. They either assume they have never really forgiven the person because the same emotions rise to the surface on occasion, or the repeated surfacing of such issues causes so much pain that they go into denial and bury their bitterness. Unconsciously they assume that genuine forgiveness is not possible in their particular situation and no final resolution ever occurs.

Forgiving is a process whereby your choice to forgive begins over time to align with your emotions.

So how does this process of "forgiving" actually work? Did you notice that Jesus tells us to love our enemies and to pray for those who persecute us, while Paul tells us twice in Romans 12:14 to *bless* those who persecute us and to *bless* and not curse. "To bless" someone can be likened to a type of prayer, and Jesus commands us directly to pray for those who have persecuted us.

The key to stage two—"forgiving"—is prayer. In the situation I alluded to earlier of being betrayed, I vowed in my heart to begin praying for this person daily. My early prayers were ones of asking God to give him what he deserved, show him the error of his ways, and cause him to repent. As time went on, the Spirit of God began to remind me of how merciful and kind He has been with me despite the evil in my heart and the things I have done. Although it was slow in coming, I eventually began to pray that God would bless the person's life, his marriage, his children, and his ministry. I made it a habit never to take the Lord's Supper until I had thoroughly and from the heart sought God's blessing on behalf of this brother.

About a year later a mutual friend visited this particular person in another state and brought back a positive report. Not knowing the depth of the betrayal that I had endured, he assumed I would be happy about the encouraging news. The initial reaction in my heart was anything but joy, but I quickly put a "Christian smile on my face" and told him how good it was to hear that this man was doing well. My first reaction told me that I was still in stage two—"forgiving." My reaction revealed that I still had subtle desires for his downfall and for justice to be meted out to him. I had forgiven him—stage one, "the choice"—but the "forgiving process" was not yet complete.

It wasn't until another eighteen months had passed (and I continued praying through this time) that through a different set of circumstances, I heard yet another positive report about this brother just minutes before I was about to preach a message at my home church. Without hesitation and without thinking, my immediate response was joy. After praying for over two years, stage two had been completed and stage three had begun!

- *Stage 3—"forgiven"—the Spirit of God aligns your choice to obey God in forgiving with the emotional experience of feeling genuine joy when blessings occur in that person's life.* It was not an easy process and I must confess that this was certainly not a onetime experience. I have had to practice these three stages of forgiveness in many situations over the years. But through this experience, I learned the three verb forms of forgiveness and experienced the peace and freedom that comes when we understand and apply genuine forgiveness.

———

I learned to bless my persecutor by praying for him and the person set free was *me*. So, how about you? Would you be willing to take a few minutes right now to ask yourself a few questions so you can begin your journey to freedom and peace?

- Who in your life do you need to forgive?
- What stage of the forgiveness process are you in?
- What lie have you believed about how forgiveness works that has held you captive?

IT'S YOUR MOVE—Become an ⊙12 Christian

I know these are very heavy questions. I encourage you to talk with a trusted friend or counselor (especially in cases of abuse) in order to start the journey of blessing those who have persecuted you. Don't let their evil infiltrate your heart.

In the next chapter we will learn some specific ways we can treat those who have hurt us so that we might experience healing within and God might demonstrate the supernatural power of goodness.

THINK—What does it mean to bless your enemy in this passage?

REFLECT—Why is forgiveness the first step in blessing the one who has hurt you?

UNDERSTAND—What stage of forgiveness are you in?

- Stage 1—the choice?
- Stage 2—the process?
- Stage 3—the completion?

SURRENDER—What is the most difficult aspect of forgiving the one who has or is aiming evil at you? Ask God to remove any bitterness and give you the strength to begin the forgiveness journey.

TAKE ACTION—Choose today to forgive the person if you have not already done so. Write it down in your Bible with today's date.

MOTIVATION—Jot down Matthew 5:43–48 on a 3×5 card or half sheet of paper. Read over it prayerfully each day for the next week.

ENCOURAGE SOMEONE—Pray today for the one who is your enemy. Choose to obey God whether you feel like it or not.

·

CHAPTER TWENTY-THREE

Do you know when you look most like Jesus?

You have heard that it was said,
"Eye for eye, and tooth for tooth."
But I tell you, Do not resist an evil person.
If someone strikes you on the right cheek,
turn to him the other also.[1]
—*Jesus of Nazareth*

Julie is fifteen and alone. She's had an abortion and just broke up with her boyfriend. Her parents split up four years ago and she has felt like a pawn going back and forth between houses ever since. She doesn't trust grown-ups now; authorities and institutions have let her down. Where was God when she cried out?

Bill is a closet homosexual raised in a rigid family. His mother was overprotective and his dad was gone most of the time, but ruled with an iron fist when home. Bill never felt close to either of them. They come from an ultrafundamentalist background where the Bible was used as a club and the God they worshipped seemed angry most of the time. Bill is living a million miles away from God right now.

Diane is a middle-aged single mom who is bitter. After over twenty years of marriage her world fell apart. Her husband's workaholism combined with her insecurities made for a bland existence for both of them. The knowledge that he was having an affair was devastating. She lost the house and was left to raise two children alone. Because the couple were prominent in their community, news spread like wildfire and her friends dropped Diane like a hot potato. She's hurt and mad and wonders where all those "church people" and God were when she needed them the most.

Don's been on the fast track for fifteen years now: successful, moderately wealthy, a rising star in the corporate world. Don is Mr. Self-Sufficient. He can do it; he thinks positively, listens to self-help CDs, works long hours, and presses hard to reach his goals. Emotionally, however, he's running on empty. He feels the pain of missing out on his kids' lives, and the marriage that looks great on the outside has moved from superficial to in trouble. Religion is for kooks and people who need a crutch in Don's mind; besides, they're all money-grabbing, sexually immoral hypocrites. He reads about them all the time in the paper.

What will it take to reach these people? What will God need to do in order to demonstrate His love to those who have given up on Him? They won't listen to your words, they won't read your Christian books, listen to your CDs, or go to church. They've been hurt and turned off. What can possibly break the stereotypes in their mind of what God and Christianity are like?

Turning Our Love into Action through Identification

The answer is found in Romans 12:14–16. As we said in the previous chapter, you are never more like Jesus than when you treat people in a way they do not deserve. We learned that we are to bless those who persecute us, to bless and curse not. This blessing begins with the choice to forgive those who have wounded, betrayed, and rejected us.

But beyond forgiving them for their actions, what does a blessing look like? How does an authentic follower move beyond the *attitude* of genuine forgiveness to specific *actions* of blessing? After commanding the Christians in Rome to "bless those who curse you; bless and do not curse" (Romans 12:14), Scripture outlines three specific commands for our behavior. The first two commands are found in verse 15: "Rejoice with those who rejoice and weep with those who weep."

Most often these verses are quoted in the context of the love and compassion believers have for one another. Although it is true that we do rejoice with those who rejoice and weep with those who weep in the Body of Christ, the context of this passage makes it clear that these actions describe how we are to bless those who are persecuting us. The truth of the matter is that we don't need a commandment to rejoice with those who rejoice when it is someone we deeply care about—we do that naturally! When a close friend or one of my children has a baby, I don't need a command to rejoice; my heart is already filled with joy. When I learn that someone I love has cancer or has lost their job, I don't need a command to weep with them; I instinctively respond with compassion and empathy because of our relationship.

"Rejoice with those who rejoice and weep with those who weep" is the practical way we are to respond to (bless) those who persecute us. Talk about counterintuitive! But before you push back your chair and mentally write me off as a lunatic, I would ask you to remember the very last words of Jesus upon the cross: "Father, forgive them, for they know not what they do." And what was it that Stephen said as he was being stoned by the Jewish religious leaders? "Father, forgive them, for they do not know what they are doing." He not only forgives them as an attitude of the heart but blesses them by his words and actions.

> We are never more like Jesus than when we are treating people in a way that they do not deserve.

You see, wholehearted identification with unbelievers is a visible manifestation of the mercy and grace of God. We are never more like Jesus than when we are treating people in a way that they do not deserve. The first step is forgiveness; and the second step is *identification*—

identifying with the pain and experiences of others. It's weeping when our persecutors weep and rejoicing when our persecutors rejoice. Can you imagine what might happen if by God's magnificent grace you followed His example and rejoiced (where appropriate*) with the joys of those who have hurt you? I've listed a few practical times that choosing to rejoice might be in order. *Rejoice with* . . .

- The birth of a baby
- Recovery from an illness
- A wedding
- A promotion
- A new home
- A long-awaited vacation
- A graduation
- The accomplishment of a long-sought-after goal.

These are all very significant events in our lives. Imagine what it would communicate if you jotted those who have hurt you a note, laughed with them, listened to their stories, asked questions about their journey, and let them relive and reexperience the joy before you. If appropriate, you could even give a gift, take them out to lunch or dinner, and pray God's blessing over their joy. If this sounds strange, consider for a moment what Jesus did. He came to His own, but His own did not receive Him (John 1:11). Nevertheless we see Him attend and rejoice at a wedding, we see Him eat and interact with His enemies, and we even see him heal members of the religious and Roman establishments that were hostile to His cause. Nothing breaks down barriers and preconceived ideas about "Christians and Christianity" more than treating people the way Jesus treated His enemies.

---

* In cases of abuse, violence, or potential danger, consult your pastor or Christian therapist, for safety issues must be paramount.

On the other side of the ledger, there are excellent opportunities to demonstrate Christ's love and forgiveness to those who persecute us during times of pain. Consider how you might respond to someone who has wounded or hurt you at . . .

- The death of a parent
- The death of a child
- The death of a friend
- The loss of a job
- A demotion
- A troubled teenager
- A troubled marriage
- A divorce
- An illness, especially cancer or something unknown
- An auto accident

What do you think it would communicate to the people who have treated you unfairly if you took time to be with them, cry with them, listen to them, send them a note, and even pray for and with them? Remember, the verse says "weep with them"; don't preach to them. *Identification is the door of love.* Don't barge your way in; let them open the door. Don't be pushy but be ready and available. The time for words will come. When we rejoice with those who rejoice and weep with those who weep, we become conduits of grace whereby good overpowers evil.

As you think through the above suggestions, I do caution you, however, to use biblical common sense and to exercise wise boundaries when necessary. Although we would like to weep with those who weep, it may be inappropriate to attempt to do so with someone who has abused you physically or sexually in the past. There also may be situations where it would be totally inappropriate to allow any kind of personal contact; yet a note or some small action that gives good for evil may well be within your power as you ask God to show you how to treat others in a way they don't deserve.

Those whom I described at the beginning of the chapter will not be moved by the size of our buildings or the tightness of logical arguments. People who have given up on God, many of whom are the kind of people who have inflicted pain on you, will only respond to God's grace when they see it coming from where they know they don't deserve it.

Be Careful of the Pharisee in All of Us

God gives a third command to help break down the walls between us and those who have attacked us. In verse 16, the command is to "live in harmony with one another." Literally this is to be "of the same mind toward one another with a focus on not being proud, but being willing to associate with the lowly." In case we missed the point, the writer follows it with this statement: "Do not be wise in your own estimation." At first blush verse 16 seems out of context with what has just been commanded. But upon careful examination I would suggest that one of the greatest dangers of applying this passage to our present relationships is a very subtle but self-righteous attitude that we are far better than others.

Left to ourselves, we tend to demonize the actions of others as deplorable and create a world where we are the good guys and anyone who has ever hurt us becomes the bad guy. We quickly excuse our faults, the times we have wounded others, pierced with our words, gossiped with our lips, or excused our bad behavior because the other person "deserved it." We're commanded to "not be haughty in mind but to associate with the lowly." There is to be no sense of superiority in our actions or attitude as we relate to those who have hurt us or those who are different from us.

How many times have you heard Christians talk about other Christians or denominations with an attitude and tone of voice that clearly communicates those they are talking about are less spiritual and inferior? The contrast to "not being haughty or arrogant in one's mind" is the next phrase, "but associate with the lowly." "Lowly" literally means "that which does not rise far above the ground, that which is base, of low degree or no status." The Apostle Paul actually uses this term to identify himself in 2 Corinthians 10:1–2. Mary praises God that He puts down rulers and exalts the *lowly* and the humble in Luke 1:52. Jesus calls Himself *lowly* and meek in Matthew 11:28–30. Isn't it ironic that Jesus the Revolutionary was comfortable with kings, beggars, prostitutes, and the social scum of the earth? And yet recent research indicates that unbelievers (especially the youth of our day) view Christians as intolerant, judgmental, hypocritical, and "unchristian."[2] So how do we turn it around? What does it look like for Christians to live like Christians when we get maligned, treated unjustly, and betrayed?

Where can we go in Scripture to learn how to forgive and bless those who have deeply wounded and persecuted us? The picture that comes to my mind is Joseph. From the time he was a young boy, his father's doting only encouraged his brothers' jealously, which led them to throw him into a pit, threaten his life, and sell him off as a slave to Egypt. Though Joseph experienced windows of God's grace, most of his prime years were spent in a damp prison, recounting the pain of being sold into slavery by his own family, falsely accused of rape, and to top it off, being forgotten by those he helped in prison.

But God had not forgotten Joseph. What people did to Joseph was wrong. It was evil. But God's good is more powerful than any evil that can be thrown at you. God is sovereign and He took the evil aimed at Joseph and used it for his good and then for the redemption of thousands of lives. At just the right time, Joseph interpreted Pharaoh's dream and became second in command to prepare Egypt and the

surrounding lands for a great famine. During this time, Joseph's enemies, his very own brothers, unknowingly collapsed at his feet and
cried for help. It was through the supernatural grace of God and many
years of healing that Joseph could tearfully look into each of his brothers' eyes and say, "You intended to harm me, but God intended it for
good to accomplish what is now being done, the saving of many lives.
So don't be afraid. I will provide for you and your children" (Genesis
50:20–21).

The life of Joseph shows us the incredible power of giving other
people what they don't deserve. As evidenced by his life, it takes significant time and great perseverance to turn people's hearts that have
become very hard. We do not have the power to change people, but we
do have the power to love them in a way that is impossible for them to
understand apart from the grace of God!

IT'S YOUR MOVE—Become an ⦾12 Christian

THINK—What in this chapter spoke to you?

REFLECT—What aspect of this teaching from Romans 12
was hardest for you to accept? Why?

UNDERSTAND—What would it look like in your situation to rejoice (or weep) with the very one who treated you
wrongly?

SURRENDER—Ask God to show you how He wants you to
apply this truth to your life in view of your specific circumstances.

TAKE ACTION—Choose from the list of actions on p. 250 and 251 and bless your enemy this week.

MOTIVATION—Download the audio message *How to Overcome the Evil Aimed at You* at **LivingontheEdge.org/r12.**

ENCOURAGE SOMEONE—Think of someone who has been betrayed or wounded unfairly and share r12 with them like Jimmy (my spiritually mature friend) did with me.

CHAPTER TWENTY-FOUR

·

Could you be "playing God" and not even know it?

But love your enemies, do good to them, and lend to them without expecting to get anything back.
Then your reward will be great,
and you will be sons of the Most High,
because he is kind to the ungrateful and wicked.
Be merciful, just as your Father is merciful.[1]
—*Jesus of Nazareth*

What do you do when you get the shaft? How do you respond
when you get a raw deal? When you're cheated on a business deal?
When someone gossips about you and spreads lies that ruin your reputation?

What are you supposed to do when someone wins the award, the
race, the trophy, or even the girl, and you know they cheated? We all
face situations in life where we've been wronged, cheated, and treated
unjustly. But as followers of Christ, how are we to respond?

In the last chapter we learned how to break the cycle of evil by blessing our persecutors. Now, as if able to read our minds, the Apostle Paul
warns us against falling into the temptation of "payback." This was my
first response when Jimmy threatened me on the basketball team in
college. After sleepless nights and uncomfortable anger inside me, I
soon came to realize the wisdom of Romans 12:17–20.

Do not repay anyone evil for evil. Be careful to do what is right in the eyes of everybody. If it is possible, as far as it depends on you, live at peace with everyone.

Do not take revenge, my friends, but leave room for God's wrath, for it is written: "It is mine to avenge; I will repay," says the Lord. On the contrary: "If your enemy is hungry, feed him; if he is thirsty, give him something to drink. In doing this, you will heap burning coals on his head."

Fighting Fire with a Gas-Filled Hose . . . It Just Doesn't Work

This passage launches into our psyche with a strong negative command—"Do not pay anyone evil for evil" or literally "*never* pay back evil for evil." And in case we missed the point in verse 17, notice the command in verse 19: "Do not take revenge my friends, but leave room for God's wrath, for it is written: 'It is mine to avenge; I will repay,' says the Lord." In other words, personal retaliation is a prohibited response for God's people.

Personal retaliation is a prohibited response for God's people.

Although everything in us wants to "pay back" those who have robbed, cheated, or hurt us, the Spirit of God clearly warns against that behavior. In fact, personal retaliation is like fighting a fire with a hose filled with gas; it only adds fuel to the fire. We may think getting back at the other person will be satisfying, but instead it escalates the conflict and pulls us into the evil itself.

After this command, the second half of verse 17 and verse 18 provide us with two specific ways to deal with people in a fallen world. The first is a preventative measure. It says, "Be careful to do what is right in the eyes of everybody." The phrase *be careful* literally means "take thought of or consider carefully what is right in the eyes of others." The New American Standard Version even translates it as "respect what is right in the eyes of all men."

As Christians, we often set ourselves up for evil by being naive. To take thought beforehand of what is right in the sight of other men helps eliminate many negative situations. We are to be shrewd as serpents but gentle as doves. We cannot ask the world or expect the world to live by our standards or ethics. The world is, in fact, incapable of doing so.

So why are we surprised at selfishness, greed, backstabbing, people not keeping their word, lying, failing to pay, betraying a confidence, or using information that we've shared with them against us? Instead, in our relationships with those outside of Christ, we need to carefully consider what is "right in their eyes." For many, lying or stealing is not a problem unless you get caught. For many, envy, jealousy, or doing whatever it takes to get what you want is simply a way of life.

We are admonished to take careful thought of how others think, re-alizing everyone acts in a way that makes sense to them. In this way we will find ourselves far less vulnerable to being on the receiving end of evil. We will all experience plenty of evil in our lifetime, but wise Christ-followers can prevent much of it by applying Paul's advice to our lives.

Our Response Reflects the God We Serve

After giving us some wisdom to prevent evil, verse 18 provides us with a prescriptive measure to reduce conflict in relationships: "If it is possible, as far as it depends on you, live at peace with everyone." No-tice that the goal is to be at peace, to live in harmony with all men—believers and unbelievers. Why? Our testimony is more important than our rights. How we respond to injustice and personal attacks is more important than getting our way or proving that we're right. This has been one of the most difficult lessons in my life. I am a "justice junkie." I don't want to let it go until everyone knows "what really happened and we make it right! Yet in the last few years I have learned the wisdom of the phrase *just let it go*. I found comfort and peace in knowing that God knows, He is just, and in a fallen world even good people do some things to you that make you scratch your head. So, let me encourage you, "Let the little stuff go." Let God handle it. Pass the ball of injustice to Him and let Him play it out as He sees fit.

But, please don't take the above advice as a membership card to become a "Christian doormat." In fact, God gives us ground rules that govern our pursuit of peace in relationships. The first is the phrase *if possible*. It's not always possible when righteousness or ethics or the welfare of others is at stake. We are not to compromise our testimony or the Lord's reputation for the sake of peace. There are times in legal situations or in family relationships when peace simply is not possible. Scripture is not advocating a "peace at any price" mentality. But it does command us to make every effort to bring about peace in our relational sphere of influence.

So the goal even in a crooked, unjust world is to seek to live in peace and harmony with those who live contrary to the truth. But there is another ground rule to consider as we seek to be agents of peace: "As far as it depends on you." It's our responsibility to ensure that antagonism and the fueling of conflict do not come from us for the sake of the Gospel. In some cases conflict is unavoidable, but make sure you're not the one inciting it. In a world of personal retaliation (road rage and domestic violence) over small things that grow into larger things, God calls us to be peacemakers whenever possible.

As I write this in my office at home, I wonder how many of us know or have relatives who no longer talk to one another because of a quarrel that started many years ago. How many workplace environments have been shattered or business relationships destroyed because evil was returned for evil. How many churches have been wrought with conflict and division rooted in personal retaliation and politics?

It is one thing to intellectually agree that "payback" is wrong, and even ungodly; but it's quite another not to do it. Even if we don't overtly seek to harm the other person, there are lots of ways that we "seek to make them pay" for how they've hurt us.

Don't Worry—God's Got You Covered

You may be much further along than I am in the faith, but I have a real problem with not retaliating when people deserve it. Few things disturb me more than injustice or evil that is willfully directed my way or toward someone I love. Everything in me wants to make it right and to pay them back now!

What has helped me most in this area are verses 19 and 20 of Romans 12. In verses 19 and 20, God provides us with two compelling reasons why we shouldn't pursue personal retaliation. First, because *you usurp God's authority and role as judge when you take retaliation into your own hands.* "Vengeance is mine," says the Lord (verse 19). "I am the judge. I will handle this situation." When you take matters into your own hands, you are taking on a job that God has already committed to do. Notice what it says: "Never take your own revenge, beloved, but leave room for the wrath of God, for it is written, 'Vengeance is mine. I will repay', says the Lord." This means God is a God of justice and will judge all men fairly and justly either in this life or in the life to come. He commands us to stay out of the boxing ring of retaliation. He's the One to carry on that fight. Once I realized that God was taking personal responsibility to make sure everyone will get exactly what they deserve—that's when I learned to "let it go."

The second reason is found in verse 20: *personal retaliation is an ineffective means to accomplish peace.* In other words, it doesn't work. At the end of the day, when I give evil for evil, it's like bad spiritual math—evil simply multiplies! Doing evil to those who have done evil to us always makes matters worse. There is only one remedy to stop evil: "If your enemy is hungry, feed him; if he is thirsty, give him something to drink. In doing this, you will heap burning coals on his head." This is a picture of what King David did with Saul in 2 Kings 6 and in 1 Samuel 24:12 when he spared Saul's life in repayment for Saul seeking to kill him.

Even evil people understand when they're not getting what they deserve. Saul, in this case, was shamed and said to David, "You are more righteous than I . . . you have treated me well, but I have treated you badly" (1 Samuel 24:17).

Saul lifted up his voice and wept. This is a picture of a man who was given good for his evil, and as a result he became aware of his own motives and felt a godly sorrow and shame. In this case, Saul's sorrow was short-lived, but it's clear from the text that God spoke in a powerful way to him through David's compassion and refusal to personally retaliate or give evil for evil.

One of the most misunderstood phrases in Romans 12 is "In doing this [giving good for evil], *you will heap burning coals on his head.*" This is not a picture of being nice to people who were mean to you so God will boil their brains out. The origin of this phrase goes back to an Egyptian ritual in which a man purged his offense by carrying on his head a dish containing burning charcoal on a bed of ashes. When someone realized they were in error, they would take coals from a fire, put them in a pan, put a towel upon their head, and carry the pan throughout the village, declaring they were burning out the bad thinking of the past. In essence, this was an act admitting their wrong and repenting of their past failure.

Loving our enemies—feeding them when they're hungry and giving them a drink when they're thirsty—is the most powerful apologetic on the face of the earth. Loving people who don't deserve to be loved in a way they don't deserve or expect can break through the hardest hearts and demonstrate the reality of the living God like few other things in the entire world.

So let me encourage you to refuse to take matters into your own hands. Refuse to give back evil for evil. Refuse to gossip about the one who has gossiped about you. Refuse to use unethical practices to pay back those who have lied to you or cheated you. Do not take your own revenge, leave room for the wrath of God. The choice is simple: either you decide that you'll handle the situation and bring about justice or you pass the ball to God and say to Him, "I'm going to let you determine what this person deserves. I'm going to treat them the way that you have treated me even though every fiber in my being wants to pay them back." Is it easy? Of course not! Does God use this to bring about peace in relationships that have been at odds for years? Absolutely!

> The choice is simple: either you decide that you'll handle the situation or you pass the ball to God.

I would like you to do some very specific thinking about how this passage applies to you. Think about some ways (even subtle ones) that you have returned evil for evil and need to repent. Ask God to give you creative ideas to express some specific acts of kindness and love to those who absolutely do not deserve it. Like David with Saul, I'd like you to honor the Word of God above your emotional feelings of betrayal and woundedness. As you do, you will experience a grace and a freedom like you have never known. The bitterness and the desire for revenge will dissipate. You can trust that full justice will occur because you have passed the responsibility of vengeance to the One True Judge who knows all aspects of the situation and by His very nature and character must be just.

As we close this chapter, a couple of questions may have come to your mind. If we are never to pay back others for what they did wrong, does this mean that we should reward bank robbers and buy steak dinners for felons? What about when we've been sold something fraudulently or someone has violated the law? Does this passage teach that we are to refrain from prosecuting them or reporting them to the government? The answer to these questions comes in our next chapter, but the

short answer is no. Romans 12 makes it clear that we are never to personally retaliate in our individual relationships; but Romans 13 is
equally clear that *God has indeed placed the government and law en-
forcement to execute justice.* The key difference is Romans 12 addresses
personal disputes, while Romans 13 addresses civil disputes and criminal behavior.

The other question that may come to your mind is simply one of
practicality. Does this really work? Won't I become a doormat if I don't
stand up for myself? How in the world can we be both strong and
Christ-like when it comes to dealing with the evil aimed at us?

In the next chapter I'll finish my story about Jimmy, the teammate
in college who threatened to kill me. I'll share with you the specific
ways to put this passage into practice whereby you will indeed see the
power of God. If we feed our enemies when they are hungry and give
them something to drink when they are thirsty, good is released in
even the vilest of relationships and has great power to transform.

IT'S YOUR MOVE—Become an Ⓡ12 Christian

THINK—Why does God prohibit personal retaliation or
revenge?

REFLECT—What happens when we pay back evil for evil?
When have you done that? What were the results?

UNDERSTAND—How can you afford to let "people off the
hook"? What is God's role? His promise?

SURRENDER—Ask God to help you turn over "justice" to Him. Pray this week, fully releasing any desire for "payback" and turn the person who has wronged you and all outcomes over to God.

TAKE ACTION—Stop saying, thinking, or hoping bad things about your enemy. Don't let these words come out of your mouth and refuse to let them linger when they come into your mind.

MOTIVATION—Consider memorizing Romans 12:19–21. Read it or say it aloud every time you're tempted to let vengeful thoughts linger or you catch yourself saying something negative about the person.

ENCOURAGE SOMEONE—Think of someone at church, work, or in the neighborhood who has been treated even more unfairly or harshly than you. Ask God to show you a tangible way to provide support to them—a note, a gift, a dinner, or a listening ear.

CHAPTER TWENTY-FIVE

Are you ready to see God do the impossible?

> "Father, forgive them, for they do not
> know what they are doing."
> And they divided up his clothes by casting lots.[1]
> —*Jesus of Nazareth*

Let's begin our time together with a game I call . . . WHAT SHOULD I DO?

Question: My boss is sexually harassing me. I've avoided him as much as possible, but he's made his intentions clear and the implications if I don't comply. But he opens all our meetings in prayer, is a leader at a local church, and even has a Bible on his desk. If he really is a brother in Christ, "am I paying back evil for evil" if I report him to the HR department?

Answer: No. The matter above is not a matter of personal retaliation, but required corporate policy. After you have spoken the truth in love ("knock it off!"), the offense is not primarily a private one, but one that involves the integrity of the company and the protection of you and others.

Question: My estranged husband left us three years ago and has not paid a penny of child support. Is it wrong to go to court or make the authorities aware of this in view of Romans 12:14–21?

Answer: No. Your husband has broken the law and it is the court's responsibility to enforce the law; it is a civil matter, not just a personal or private issue. Your attitude toward your estranged husband is a Romans 12 issue; his delinquency in child support is a Romans 13 issue.

In both cases above, there is a Romans 12 and Romans 13 application. Romans 12 is directed toward the prohibition of personal retaliation and revenge for a wound or hurt inflicted. We are to bless those who curse us; refuse to pay back evil for evil; and do good to those who have done evil to us. This is a countercultural response to personal attack and requires much grace; but when it is obeyed, it will protect you from the poison of bitterness and will release God's power to work in the heart of your persecutor.

By contrast, Romans 13 addresses how God brings about justice in civil and/or criminal matters:

> *Everyone must submit himself to the governing authorities, for there is no authority except that which God has established. The authorities that exist have been established by God. Consequently, he who rebels against the authority is rebelling against what God has instituted, and those who do so will bring judgment on themselves.*
>
> *For rulers hold no terror for those who do right, but for those who do wrong. Do you want to be free from fear of the one in authority? Then do what is right and he will commend you. For he is God's servant to do you good. But if you do wrong, be afraid, for he does not bear the sword for nothing. He is God's servant, an agent of wrath to bring punishment on the wrongdoer.*

Situations become even more difficult when they involve both private and civil/criminal issues. There are times we must make sure our heart is right, forgive the offender, and even seek to do good unto them when possible, while at the same time press charges, report criminal behavior, or exercise provisions under the law.

A great example of this occurred recently in an Amish community that was the victim of a deranged gunman. In a moment of despair, he took hostages in their small school. The Amish called on the authorities (police) to execute justice and attempt to free the hostages. They fully cooperated with the police in their attempts to rescue the children. The gunman eventually killed seven or eight little girls and was later killed himself. In actions that stunned the media, the Amish leaders later openly forgave the gunman and prayed for his wife and family after he was killed. In this situation they responded to the evil aimed at them in obedience to both Romans 12 and 13. If you have thorny questions on when to apply Romans 12 or Romans 13, I encourage you to talk with your pastor or another mature Christian about your situation.

Whatever Happened to Jimmy?

As we bring the final chapter of this book to a close (but just beginning our journey), there are two questions that need to be answered:

1. Does this r12 "supernaturally responding to evil with good" *really* work?
2. Whatever happened with Jimmy—the guy who threatened to kill you?

The best way to answer both of these questions is to finish the story. Jimmy, you will remember was the big, six-six ex-con, "reformed" drug addict and dealer who described himself as evil, had a scar from one shoulder blade completely around his body to his chest from Vietnam, and hated all Christians . . . and *me* in particular!

My response prior to learning God's will in Romans 12:14–21 was to repay evil for evil. I was bitter, consumed with hate, living in fear, and at a complete loss as to what I should do. Into that situation God used another man named Jimmy (God has a sense of humor!) to walk me through what I shared with you in these last five chapters. Understanding what to do was only 10 percent of the battle; it was the other 90 percent of being *willing* to give good for evil to a man I hated that was so painfully difficult!

"Obedience is a choice," my friend Jimmy reminded me. "You don't have to feel like obeying, you just choose to do it, and you'll discover God's grace will be sufficient every time."

Well, I certainly didn't feel like it or even want to do it; but I obeyed . . .

> . . . no more behind-the-back passes
> . . . no more no-look-in-your-face assists
> . . . no more sarcasm
> . . . no more rejoicing when he messed up
> . . . no more telling other players and other people what a jerk
>   he was

Those are the things that I stopped doing (at least the ones I can share publicly). But the passage doesn't merely say, "Don't pay back evil for evil," it goes on to say, "If your enemy is thirsty, give him something to drink; if he is hungry, give him something to eat . . . do not be overcome with evil *but overcome evil with good!*"

So doing good to Jimmy was the next act of *obedience*. As a freshman on a college basketball team, you are at the mercy of the upperclassmen. "Put my bag on the bus" "Go get me a Coke!" "Wait in line for me," etc., etc., etc. Well, Jimmy used those privileges to make me his personal slave. He knew it got to me and I hated every moment of it. So, that seemed like the first place to begin this new "doing good for evil" experiment.

For the next four months Jimmy never had to ask. "Hey, Jimmy, I've got your bag, I put it on the bus; anything else I can get for you?"

"Jimmy, I'm going back for seconds [at the team meal], can I get you a Coke or another piece of meat?"

When Jimmy went to the shower, I gathered his sweaty practice gear, put it in the nylon bag, gave it to the trainer to be washed, and then folded his clothes next to his locker.

Week after week, month after month, I did good for evil. The teasing and the humiliation did *not* stop. His hatred even seemed to intensify at times. Once he asked if I was trying some "Christian trick" to get him to leave me alone. By God's grace I just kept doing good; it actually became my personal challenge to do something good every day for Jimmy.

To my amazement, within a couple of weeks, one big thing changed—me! The anger and bitterness melted away. His insults and words lost their power (though I still disliked it); the sting was gone! I started praying regularly for Jimmy as part of my "bless him" part of the equation, and I began to see Jimmy through new eyes. I saw an extremely talented, bitter, angry man who blamed God for all his problems. I even caught myself on occasion feeling sorry for Jimmy. He was miserable, but I could never see that until I stopped hating him.

> To my amazement, one big thing changed—me!

I'd love to end this story by telling you how Jimmy was struck by the love of God, bent his knee at half-court, and asked Jesus to be his Savior, but I can't—it didn't happen that way.

No, we came to the end of the season and nothing changed . . . at least not anything I could see. It was after our final game in a big year-end conference tournament that Jimmy turned to me and said words I will never forget.

"Chee-up, there are only two people on this team that I respect: *me*—'cause I am evil and I know it and I'm on my way to hell if there is one . . . and *you*! I disagree with every single thing you say and believe, but if I was ever in any way going to become a Christian, I'd have to say that I'd want to be one like you."

Then he added, "I'm done messin' with your mind, kid; I'll leave you alone." I was in shock; I thanked him and saw for the first time in his eyes that his hatred for me was gone. I wish there was a happy end-ing to the story, but I never knew for sure what happened to Jimmy. I heard he got picked up on a drug charge and went back to prison, but I really don't know.

What I do know is that good is more powerful than evil! It is possible by God's grace to love our enemies. God can change the hardest of hearts. It does work!

Now it's *your* turn . . .

IT'S YOUR MOVE—Become an ⊙l2 Christian

THINK—What does it mean to be an r12 Christian?

REFLECT—How has this r12 journey impacted your life?

UNDERSTAND—Of the five relationships we have studied together, in which of these have you seen the greatest spiritual growth? In which area do you need the most help in becoming more like Christ?

- Relationship with God
- Relationship to the world system
- Relationship with yourself
- Relationship with believers
- Relationships with unbelievers

SURRENDER—Surrender is a point in time and also a lifelong journey. How would you describe your present relationship to God?

- "I'm all in!"
- "I'm holding back just a little."
- "I need help, I'm stuck concerning . . ."

TAKE ACTION—This book is just the beginning of becoming an r12 Christian.

MOTIVATION—If you commit to becoming an r12 disciple maker, go to **LivingontheEdge.org/r12** and explore our free resources to help you disciple others.

ENCOURAGE SOMEONE—Encourage someone you know in another city who wants to grow. Send them a copy of this book and coach them or do the study with them.

B.I.O.
(BEFORE GOD DAILY, IN COMMUNITY WEEKLY, ON MISSION 24/7)

B.I.O. is the pathway to becoming an R12 disciple.

BEFORE GOD DAILY

Our tendency is to bury our wounds, suppress our hurts, and live with a deep-seated bitterness. But bitterness and hatred are like a cancer that eats away at our souls. Someone once said that harboring bitterness is like drinking poison and hoping the other person gets sick. When we refuse to forgive, the person we end up hurting the most is ourselves.

Part of our healing happens as we learn to come before God. When we come before God and spend time in His Word, we are regularly confronted with his command to forgive and to even bless those who have hurt us. We are also reminded that God is in control and that we can trust Him. God is a God of justice, and in His own time He will make things right.

One of the ways that Jesus told us to bless those who have hurt us is by praying for them. If you are carrying a grudge, when you come before God in the coming days make it a point to pray for that person.

Earlier in this section I challenged you to write out Matthew 5:43–48 on some 3x5 cards and read over them prayerfully each day for the next week. If you haven't already done this exercise, do so this next week.

IN COMMUNITY WEEKLY

In this section, I wrote about my teammate Jimmy. His relentless badgering and harassing caused me to hate him. I shared my situation with a friend who was helping lead our college ministry. My friend was wise enough to point me to this passage in Romans 12. I will never forget his words: "There is only one thing I know that is more powerful than this kind of evil, and it is the good that comes from God."

It was an incredible gift to have a friend point me to Scripture and to challenge me to overcome evil with good. My friend is a good example of why we all need to be in community with other believers. Solomon said that "an honest answer is like a kiss of friendship" (Proverbs 24:26 NIV). It may not feel like it at that time, but having people in your life who tell you the truth and challenge you to obedience truly is a gift from God.

ON MISSION 24/7

This passage in Romans 12:14–21 calls on us to "rejoice with those who rejoice and weep with those who weep." The context of the passage makes it clear that these actions describe how we are to bless those who persecute us and have hurt us.

When you are on mission, you don't just forgive in your heart, you actually take steps to reach out to those who have hurt you. And one way to do that is by identifying with them in their own life situations. As I wrote in this section, "identification is the door of love." I gave you several possible actions on page 251. Select one of those actions and demonstrate God's love this week to someone who has wounded you in the past. Be the conduit of extravagant grace and radical love.

The Journey Continued . . .

Thank you for allowing me to join you on your spiritual pilgrimage. Although we will never be perfect in this life, it is God's passionate desire to continually transform our hearts and lives to reflect the beauty, love, and holiness of Jesus.

His purposes are always for our good but even more to display the infinite wonders of His grace, wisdom, love, and power, so that our lives cry out, "Holy, holy, holy is the Lord God Almighty, who was and is, and is to come."

My prayer is that you will grasp how greatly you are loved and live out an r12 relational lifestyle—not to earn God's favor but to say thank you for what He has already done.

The journey is ongoing . . .

. . . surrender to God
. . . separation from the world's values
. . . sober self-assessment
. . . serving of others in love
. . . supernatural response to evil with good

. . . and will never end until He comes or we are called home to heaven.

In the meantime, imagine what our great God and Savior Jesus will do in every circumstance and relationship as we become r12 Christians 24/7, 365 days a year!

And the things you have heard me say in the presence of many witnesses entrust to reliable men who will also be qualified to teach others.

—2 TIMOTHY 2:2

Keep pressin' ahead—
Chip

Remember, Jesus' number one priority for every area of your life: *You BELIEVE in God . . . TRUST also in ME!*

—JOHN 14:1

·

A Word to Pastors

In the last several years I've had the privilege to crisscross America and go around the world to minister with fellow pastors who long to see their churches produce Christ-like followers who live out their faith day in and day out.

It is no secret that something is terribly wrong. Most Christians do not live like Christians. Most churches (with wonderful but rare exceptions) are struggling. Pastors from all backgrounds admit they do not have a definition of the question "What is a disciple of Jesus Christ?" And few churches have a clear, systematic process for maturing their members.

This book is my hope and prayer to partner with pastors everywhere to help you not only define but develop grace-filled, winsomely holy, and loving followers of Jesus Christ.

You don't have to take my word for it. In case any of us need any more motivation or doubt the critical nature of this issue, I want to share four quotes from Christian leaders whom God used to keep the fire burning in my soul.

A voice from the past looking at the priority of spiritual maturity sixty years ago . . .

> *Our most pressing obligation today is to do all in our power to ob-tain a revival that will result in a reformed, revitalized, purified church. It is of far greater importance that we have better Chris-tians than we have more of them. Each generation of Christians is the seed of the next, and degenerate seed is sure to produce a degen-erate harvest not a little better than but a little worse than the seed from which it sprang. Thus the direction will be down until vigor-ous, effective means are taken to improve the seed. . . .*
>
> *To carry on these activities [evangelism, missions] scripturally the church should be walking in fullness of power, separated, puri-fied and ready at any moment to give up everything, even life itself, for the greater glory of Christ. For a worldly, weak, decadent church to make converts is but to bring forth after her own kind and ex-tend her weakness and decadence a bit farther out. . . .*
>
> *So vitally important is spiritual quality that it is hardly too much to suggest that attempts to grow larger might well be sus-pended until we have become better.*[1]
>
> —A. W. TOZER

A voice of today from a man who has spent every summer for the past fifteen years traveling around the world to "take the church's spiritual temperature" . . .

> *Q: You know this growing church probably as well as any Westerner does. I wonder how you evaluate it.*
>
> *John Stott:* The answer is "growth without depth." None of us wants to dispute the extraordinary growth of the church. But it has

been largely numerical and statistical growth. And there has not been sufficient growth in discipleship that is comparable to the growth in numbers.

Q: *Where do we evangelicals need to go? We've been through quite a trip in the last fifty years.*

John Stott: My immediate answer is that we need to go beyond evangelism. Evangelism is supposed to be evangelicals' specialty. Now, I am totally committed to world evangelization. But we must look beyond evangelism to the transforming power of the gospel, both in individuals and in society.[2]

A megachurch's self-assessment after twenty-five years of ministry . . .

But the research findings are also extremely clear, *the church should do everything it can to increase the number of those who are fully surrendered followers of Jesus Christ* . . . the potential for Kingdom impact is huge.[3]

The most recent empirical research on the lifestyle and behaviors of those who claim the name of Christ . . .

We consistently find that the vast majority of teenagers nationwide will spend a significant amount of their teen years participating in a Christian congregation. Most teenagers in America enter adulthood considering themselves to be Christians and saying they have made a personal commitment to Christ. But within a decade, most of these young people will have left the church and will have placed emotional connection to Christianity on the shelf. For most of them their faith was merely skin-deep. This leads to the sobering finding that the vast majority of outsiders in this country, particularly among young generations, are actually de-churched individuals.

A Proven Pathway to Becoming Like Jesus

You see, we've got a problem. And it breaks my heart—which is why I wrote this book. So, here's the question: Will you be part of the solution? Will you let God transform your life in such a way that it is a magnet for those who don't know Christ? Will you become an r12 Christian? Will you surrender your life to God? Will you become separate from the world? Will you have a sober self-assessment? Will you serve others in love? Will you supernaturally respond to evil with good?

If you follow this simple (but by no means easy) pathway, God will start to transform your life. He is ready to use you to lead in helping to transform His people into r12 Christians. Will you answer His call?

Endnotes

CHAPTER ONE: What does God really want from you?

1. A. W. Tozer, *The Knowledge of the Holy* (New York: Harper & Row, 1961), 83.
2. Matthew 11:28 NIV.

CHAPTER TWO: Why is it so hard to surrender to God?

1. Matthew 11:29 NIV.
2. The book *Risk, Reason, and the Decision-Making Process* is fictitious. I created the stories and case studies as a present-day parable to help us recalibrate our view of commitment and surrender as Jesus did in Matthew 13:44–45. All further stories/books are historical.

CHAPTER THREE: Do you believe God has your best in mind?

1. Matthew 11:30 NIV.

CHAPTER FOUR: What does a surrendered life look like?

1. John 12:24 NIV.

CHAPTER FIVE: Are you "all in"?

1. Matthew 6:24 NIV.

CHAPTER SIX: Are you getting God's best?

1. Tozer, *The Knowledge of the Holy,* 84.
2. Luke 9:23–24 NIV.

CHAPTER SEVEN: Why is the Christian life so difficult?

1. Luke 9:25 NIV.

CHAPTER EIGHT: Are you a faithful lover?

1. Matthew 4:1–3.
2. R. Warren, Message by Rick Warren, Monterey, CA. Delivered at the Half Time Conference, October 2006.
3. D. Kinnaman and G. Lyons, *unChristian* (Grand Rapids: Baker, 2007).

CHAPTER NINE: Could your mental diet be killing your soul?

1. Matthew 4:4 NIV.

CHAPTER TEN: Are you tired of "trying hard" and feeling guilty?

1. John 8:31–32 NIV.

CHAPTER ELEVEN: Who do you think you are?

1. Tozer, *The Knowledge of the Holy,* 104.
2. Luke 14:11 NIV.

CHAPTER TWELVE: Have you answered life's biggest questions?

1. Luke 16:15 NIV.

CHAPTER THIRTEEN: Have you discovered the real you?

1. John 10:27–28 NIV.
2. W. R. Newell, *Romans Verse by Verse* (Chicago: Moody Press, 1952).

CHAPTER FOURTEEN: Where do you fit in God's family?
1. Luke 12:48 NIV.

CHAPTER FIFTEEN: Do you know God's
purpose for your life?
1. Matthew 25:23 NIV.

CHAPTER SIXTEEN: What is authentic community anyway?
1. Tozer, *The Knowledge of the Holy,* 63.

CHAPTER SEVENTEEN: Why is God so serious
about your authenticity?
1. John 13:34–35 NIV.

CHAPTER EIGHTEEN: Are you building relationships
that will last a lifetime?
1. John 15:12–13 NIV.

CHAPTER NINETEEN: What's keeping you from
experiencing authentic community?
1. John 5:44 NIV.

CHAPTER TWENTY: Where's your focus?
1. John 17:20–21.

CHAPTER TWENTY-ONE: Who has hurt you the most?
1. Tozer, *The Knowledge of the Holy,* 106.
2. Matthew 5:43–44.

CHAPTER TWENTY-TWO: Will you let Christ heal you?
1. Matthew 6:14–15.
2. R. T. Kendall, *Total Forgiveness* (Lake Mary: Charisma House).

CHAPTER TWENTY-THREE: Do you know when you look most like Jesus?

1. Matthew 5:38–39 NIV.
2. Kinnaman and Lyons, *unChristian*.

CHAPTER TWENTY-FOUR: Could you be "playing God" and not even know it?

1. Luke 6:35–36 NIV.

CHAPTER TWENTY-FIVE: Are you ready to see God do the impossible?

1. Luke 23:34.

APPENDIX: A Word to Pastors

1. A. W. Tozer, *The Set of the Sail* (Camp Hill, PA: Wingspread, 1986), 154–56.
2. John Stott Interview by Tim Stafford, "Evangelism Plus," in *Christianity Today*, October 2006.
3. G. Hawkins and C. Parkinson, *Reveal: Where Are You?* (Barrington, IL: Willow Creek, 2007).

Next Steps to Living on the Edge...

Connect Online...

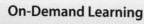 online
true spirituality™

On-Demand Learning

If you have questions about how to grow deeper as an r12 Christian, go online and study at your own pace in a video-rich experience.

Connect in Groups...

Small Group Study

What did Jesus say about being an r12 Christian? How did He model it? This small group study includes six 15-minute videos taught by Chip Ingram.

Connect your Church...

r12 | church
true spirituality™

Church-Wide Teaching & Study Series

Is your church body becoming more like Jesus? Learn how your church can grow as more authentic disciples by becoming an r12 church.

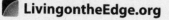

LivingontheEdge.org